D1373632

FRANCIS WARNER
poet and dramatist

Courtesy of Oxford Mail & Times

FRANCIS WARNER
poet and dramatist

edited by
Tim Prentki

Sceptre Press

First published in 1977 by
Sceptre Press
Knotting, Bedfordshire

ISBN 0 7068 0378 7

Printed in Great Britain
by W & J Mackay Limited, Chatham

Contents

Books by Francis Warner

Poetry

Perennia. Cambridge, Golden Head Press, 1962.
Early Poems. London, Fortune Press, 1964.
Experimental Sonnets. London, Fortune Press, 1965.
Madrigals. London, Fortune Press, 1967.
The Poetry of Francis Warner. Boston, Mass., Pilgrim Press, 1970.
Meeting Ends. Knotting, Bedfordshire, Sceptre Press, 1973.
Lucca Quartet. Knotting, Omphalos Press, 1975.

Plays

Maquettes, a trilogy of one-act plays. Oxford, Carcanet Press, 1972.
   (Oxford Theatre Texts 1.)
Lying Figures (Part one of REQUIEM, a trilogy). Oxford, Carcanet
   Press, 1972. (Oxford Theatre Texts 2.)
Killing Time (Part two of REQUIEM). Cheadle, Carcanet Press,
   1976. (Oxford Theatre Texts 3.)
Meeting Ends (Part three of REQUIEM). Cheadle, Carcanet Press,
   1974. (Oxford Theatre Texts 4.)

Editor

Eleven Poems by Edmund Blunden. Cambridge, Golden Head Press,
   1965.
Garland. Cambridge, Golden Head Press, 1968.
Studies in the Arts. Oxford, Basil Blackwell, 1968.
De Occulta Philosophia, Libri tres, by H. Cornelius Agrippa, a biblio-
   graphical edition. (In preparation.)

Preface

Since the collection of poetry that won him the Messing International Award for Literature in 1972, Francis Warner has written a series of plays, performed at four Edinburgh Festivals, which have won considerable acclaim, making him perhaps, in the verdict of Sir Harold Hobson in this book, 'the most remarkable of those dramatists of our time who have striven to push the limits of theatre beyond their age-old limits'.

It is hoped that this collection of essays by professional scholars or those professionally involved with the theatre, published for his fortieth birthday, will go some way towards preparing new audiences of his plays and new readers of his poetry for an understanding of his achievement.

All the contributors have known Mr Warner's work for many years, and I should like to thank them for their help and encouragement in the preparation of this volume. Special thanks are due to A. H. Buck for his work in reading the proofs.

TIM PRENTKI

Oxford, 1977

Note to 'The Language of Francis Warner'

Francis Warner's published works have been systematically read for the new *Supplement to the Oxford English Dictionary* (Vol. I, A–G, 1972, Vol. II, H–N, 1976), with which the writers of this piece have been associated. A number of the quotations obtained from this reading have made their way into the relevant entries in the Supplement, for example, s.v. *Interflora* (*M* 30), *it* (*M* 16), *kinky* (*LF* 3.36), *lover boy* (*LF* 2.9), and *mini-skirted* (*M* 19). It seems to us likely that he is quoted in the Supplement as often as, say, Thomas Campion and John Clare are quoted in the parent work, the *O.E.D.* itself.

EP	*Early Poems*	M	*Maquettes*
ES	*Experimental Sonnets*	M:E	*Emblems*
KT	*Killing Time*	M:T	*Troat*
LF	*Lying Figures*	M:L	*Lumen*
LQ	*Lucca Quartet*	Mad.	*Madrigals*
	ME	*Meeting Ends*	

LESLEY BURNETT
ROBERT BURCHFIELD

1

Lesley Burnett and Robert Burchfield

The Language of Francis Warner

I THE POETRY

The traditionalism of Francis Warner's poems contrasts strikingly with the modernism of his plays. As one would expect, the influence of other poets is most manifest in *EP* (1964). His prevalent sensuousness, lover's idealism, and, above all, verbal music recall Yeats, while, at the other historical extreme, 'My Patient Pen' (*EP*, 28–29) bears Wyatt's stamp. In 'Lyric' (*EP*, 34) the simple diction, the use of Nature as a metaphorical analogue for decaying love, the naming of the place 'Madingley Hill', and the steady, almost indifferent tone and pace sustained to an ending of sober resignation create a mood typical of Hardy. The sentiments of 'Castle Leslie' (*EP*, 12) are precisely those central to Wordsworth's idea of emotion recollected in tranquillity. In the longest poem of the collection, 'Perennia' (41–65), the modulations of the Spenserian stanza are controlled with sensitive assurance, a Keatsian sensuous density and delicacy is blended with a Tennysonian languor, and there are even more traditional elements in its dream-vision, such as the catalogues of birds, animals, and precious stones. *Madrigals* (1967) reverts to the style of *EP*: 'The Passionate Goatherd' (*Mad.*, 7) is an adaptation, and a very close one, of Marlowe's celebrated lyric, 'Come live with me, and be my love', and 'Impromptu' (8) and 'Close, close tight buds' (17) could well have been written by Campion for the accompaniment of the lute; even after *Experimental Sonnets* (1965), 'Sonnet' (*Mad.*, 9) is distinctly Shakespearian; and the main themes remain Nature in its varying moods, friendship, solitary observation, places, and love, both ecstatic and evanescent.

What this variety of influence really indicates is, not that Mr Warner copies poets, but that he writes lyrics of individual stature which show a highly accomplished craftsmanship. He writes in the *spirit* of others, but the poems remain decidedly his

own, showing a serious and humble sympathy with the imagina-
tions of great writers that in less committed minds would produce
only parody.

The last two poems in *EP*, 'A Legend's Carol' (66–71) and
'Plainsong' (72–80), anticipate the kind of originality found in
ES (1965). The former poem celebrates the nativity in realistic
terms appropriate to the twentieth century, but the gentle
harmonies of its original stanza and the blending of the tradi-
tional with the modern in its treatment of its theme ensure that
it never has to sacrifice the tender idealism and domesticity of
pastoral, as Eliot's 'Journey of the Magi' does. The latter poem
is a latter-day 'Lycidas'—aptly disturbed in verse-form, rest-
lessly ranging in time and place, violent and gentle by turns,
and personal without being exclusive. These two poems con-
stitute a stylistic shattering of the leaves for Mr Warner: the
formal originality of frequently bringing rhyme from the ends
of lines to the middles in *Experimental Sonnets* is characteristic of
the new tone—direct and masculine, toughly energetic, realistic
—that they announce.

With the exception of the *Experimental Sonnets*, virtually all of
Mr Warner's poems are preoccupied with the music of words,
and their simple, modest, and yet often moving lyricism is
readily adaptable to the demands of song. Music metaphors are
central to the expression of several poems ('Threshold', *EP*, 33;
Sonnets XVIII and XXII, *ES*, 24, 28), and the very titles of
some of the poems near the end of *Madrigals* disclose the sug-
gestion of a musical background—'The Ballad of Brendan
Behan', 'East Coast Calypso', 'West Coast Blues'. It comes as
no surprise, therefore, that 'A Legend's Carol' (*EP*, 66–71) has
been set to music by Leon Coates. The close of 'Camaiore', the
first poem in Mr Warner's latest booklet, *Lucca Quartet* (1975),
harmonizes its alliterative, iterative, rhyming, and rhythmic
devices into a lulling benediction with the grace and innocence
of a children's hymn:

> May wings stretch over you
>   Spring touch your vein
> Loveliness lighten
>   To childhood again
> Falling hair fasten
>   Love to your breast

By Florentine scentfall
            Caressed.

The word 'scentfall' in this example, subtly releasing the
bouquet of 'Florentine', shows another pervasive characteristic
of Mr Warner's poetic language: compound words. These serve
two basic functions: to enrich sensuousness by awakening
wonder at new sensations; and to contain anguish or deep feel-
ing bursting for expression. In general, these two uses character-
ize Mr Warner's two basic styles, that already found in *EP*,
Mad., and *LQ*, and that in *ES*. In 'Perennia' (*EP*, 41–65) com-
pound adjectives in particular promote the poem's atmosphere
of heavy exotic dreaminess: 'wine-filled blackberry', 'the stream-
bound dragon-fly', 'the sun-turned tree-top branches', 'the
cloud-flecked summer sky', 'the rain-filled hedges', 'dew-
drenched gold'. In *Mad.* we find 'gull-soft cheeks' (19), and in
'Camaiore' in *LQ* even ordinary compounds such as 'afternoon',
'sunbeams', 'wildwood', 'hillside', 'pinetree', 'farmyards', and
'weather-worn' exemplify a simple nomenclature which cor-
relates with primitive pastoral feeling. By contrast, the com-
pounds in *ES* are fraught with tougher emotion, as some of the
nouns will illustrate: 'eunuch-mystic's incense-smoke' (9), 'fever-
bout' (10), 'butcher-doubts' (17), 'carcass-thief' (21). Though
some adjectives of the kind already found elsewhere in the poetry
continue Mr Warner's sensuous, descriptive mode—'feather-
breath tangent of God', 'moss-bearded waterfall', 'song-
drenched accolade' (18, 20, 21)—others show the trend set by
the nouns—'nutcracked knees', 'nonsense-babbling talk' (11,
26). When in Sonnet X, driving along a country road at night—

> The headlights catch the cautious rabbits' play
> And romp them roadsiding, to widow past,
> Unkiss the shroud and lift the latch of dark;
> Probing the bosomed, catseyed mist ahead
> Half-formed and damp; thick, intermittent, gone.
> This far-past-midnight world of deerhorned trunks
> And unrepentant fields so utterly ours
> We tread the edge of promise with the dawn.

—the unusual compounds 'roadsiding', 'catseyed', 'far-past-
midnight', and 'deerhorned' exactly catch the strange, spectral

unreality of the experience. In 'Plainsong' (*EP*, 72–80), com-
pounds such as 'mind-spider', 'dream-stifled', 'tempest-dance',
'walrus-wastes', 'zoo-beast', 'meadow-grazer', and 'razor-cut'
almost trenchantly represent harsh reality in a way that heralds
the concerns, and the tone, of the *Sonnets*. In *Madrigals* the
compounds in 'When You Are Mine' (10)—'the stud-gripped
fastener', 'the knee-raised stocking'—are used to reveal familiar-
ity with fixed erotic images.

Mr Warner's creativity in vocabulary is not confined to com-
pounds. Sometimes he freshens the meaning of a conventional
adjective by using a slightly unconventional form: 'chaosed
winds', 'cycloning minds' (*ES*, 14), 'baritoned . . . waterfall'
(*ES*, 20). More usually, he extends the meaning of an existing
word. A *girasole* is an opal which reflects a reddish glow in bright
light, but when he speaks of 'this . . . girasole of leaf' in autumn
(*Mad.*, 23), he exactly pictures autumn leaves, perhaps bluish-
white with decay or by being turned in the wind, giving a reddish
glow in the sun. When in 'The Statues' (*Mad.*, 19) he says
'*Recondition* was my need', he is able to associate the wish for
deep learning with one for healing and secrecy, and by using
'trans-sanity' (*EP*, 80) he is able to refer to a highly enlightened
state of mind beyond sanity which, by being non-human, is
perhaps not entirely desirable. Mr Warner also coins verbs:
'cynicize', meaning to think cynically, 'granite', meaning to
sharpen on granite, and 'bark up', meaning to cause a dog to
start barking (*ES*, 13, 25; *Mad.*, 21). The verb in the line
'Contorted, grotesque, like shadows that camp-fire the night'
(*EP*, 75), taken from the noun and made transitive, aptly con-
torts ordinary reality, and reinforces the paradox whereby
shadows (dark, frighteningly insubstantial) act as a camp-fire
(normally cosy, protective, the focus of human society) to the
night. The verb *cataract* in the lines

> [like] madmen leaning on a laddered man
> Who gazes frantic at the swimming ground
> While stifling heart-pants cataract his eyes (*EP*, 76)

means to give cataracts to the eyes, but, especially in the con-
text of *swimming*, describes the flooding of vision with a fall from
a height.

It is clear that Mr Warner's creativity is at its most intense in expressing deep, anguished emotion, for it is then that he must find, somehow, the words for essentially wordless feeling. It is therefore significant that his verbal invention is at its peak in the *Experimental Sonnets* and in the last two poems of *Early Poems*, for it is in these poems that he is most concerned with violent action and reaction, and necessarily with the body, as the medical words 'cancered', 'cataract', 'vivisecting', 'fever-bout', and 'nervepoint' reveal (*EP*, 76; *ES*, 7, 10, 18). When he uses the expression 'to cauterize his love' in 'Perennia' (*EP*, 55), the verb is altogether too technical, too medical and painful, for the idyllic atmosphere, just as 'mentor' in the same work (45) is too modern, and too American, in its associations.

Vocabulary is often carefully chosen within single poems, for example, in 'Canzone' (*LQ*). The poem opens in light self-mockery:

> Here sits the chess-set, silenced *in flagrante*
> When your self-mocking anger
> Mated checked love and challenged concentration.

The punning chess metaphor, so typical of Mr Warner's technique in his plays, is here functioning, with the grandiose *in flagrante*, in establishing the tone with tart good-humour. Italianate words—'Carracci's Baccante', 'the Urbino Venus'— give an appropriate foreign flavour, but the fact that they are set in the immediate context of 'Mother shocked stiff', 'the Elvis record', and 'Lucy's[1] sweet welcome crayoned for your break-fast' characterizes the Italian holiday as a mixture of the self-consciously idealistic (the Elvis record is 'our reveille' and the characters have preserved the 'trophies' of their 'climbing zest') and the very ordinary. From this Mr Warner very skilfully moulds a statement of idealism in love, by using Latin and Greek vocabulary in the second part of the poem with increasing seriousness: 'trepidation . . . exhilaration . . . spontaneous . . . anathemata . . . cantata . . . catastrophe . . . ecstasy'. Thus the poem virtually changes gear in the middle, and though it begins with 'Here sits the chess-set, silenced *in flagrante*' and ends within 26 lines with 'and breed proud children in shared ecstasy', it is

---

[1] Lucy is Mr Warner's younger daughter. His elder daughter, also referred to in *Lucca Quartet* (though not by name), is the subject of 'For Georgina' (*Mad.*, 18).

unified by its consistent selection of vocabulary, first used in mockery, but finally in proud, elevated resolution.

It is very unusual indeed, when one remembers that such finesse is typical, to come across poor writing in Mr Warner's poems; but one little simile from 'Camaiore' (*LQ*) is persistently niggling:

> Smoke curls
> From a weather-worn building
> Tiled in sun
> Like your cheeks when happiness
> Is done.

The building 'Tiled in sun' resembles his lover's cheeks after love-making, flushed, reddish-pale, yes; but the details of the simile obtrude unfortunately. Is she 'weather-worn', really like a building, or 'tiled' in the cheeks? The smoke curling from the building even suggests that she has a smoke after love-making— a bit banal for idyllic celebration, let alone compliment. Every simile, it is true, has an element of 'not-like' as well as 'like' in it, but it seems that Mr Warner has not sufficiently governed the 'not-like' in this instance.

In general, however, it is clear from Mr Warner's poetry that he has both a sound, sympathetic grip on traditional English poetry and an individual creativity, that he is able to write gently or trenchantly, musically or harshly, as his subject seems to demand, that he exhibits a considerable metrical variety, and that, in such poems as those at the close of *EP*, he is able to combine these different modes in one composition. This omens well for the future.

II THE PLAYS

Turning from the poetry to the plays, one encounters something of a shock, though one had been prepared for the preoccupations and the harshness of the drama in *ES*, XXII: 'Bear with me if I leave such scenes behind: / The dark offstage preoccupies my mind.' Indeed, the earlier poems are frequently incorporated into the plays (for example, *M:L*, 46, quotes *Mad.*, 14; *LF*, 4. 39, quotes *Mad.*, 13), where they form transitory points of rest and hope contrasting with the brutality and despair of the main body of the text. Scattered throughout the plays are other fairly self-contained poems, mostly in the idyllic mood and style of the early works, and employing similar compound words: 'green-gold laughter' (*KT*, 1.10.31), 'day-dull thoughts' (*ibid.*) 'fresh-lost music' (*ME*, 1.9.31), 'light-pinned stars' (*ibid.*). In general, the plays fall naturally into movements (the musical structure being intentional), the 'poetic' style alternating with a very different, colloquial, down-to-earth mode of writing. In addition, the plays have a concern with symbolic action which is not typical of the poetry.

The most striking items of vocabulary in the plays are names. The characters in *M* are rendered generic by their anonymity, but thereafter symbolic and significant naming is employed. For heuristic purposes the names can be divided into three rough categories, though of course there is a good deal of overlap:

1. Those which are *appropriate* to the character. Such are, for example, Guppy in *LF* (a small fish) or Squaloid in *KT* (shark-like). Squaloid's predatory and scavenging actions speak for themselves, and his name also contains a judgement upon them in its resemblance to 'squalid'. It is quite common for the sound of names in this category to be expressive.

2. Those which concern the audience's interpretation of the character's significance, but also add to and extend the sphere of action. Such, for example is Agappy in *ME* (*agape*, Christian love, frequently contrasted with earthly or sexual love) and Ensoff in the same play, whose dress and position on the stage 'high up on a raised platform . . . that is quite separate from the main circular acting area' (1.1) make clear his symbolic significance, but who is also En-Soph or En-Sof, the absolute infinite and incomprehensible god in Cabbalistic doctrine.

3. Those in which ignorance of the meaning of the character's name is a considerable obstacle to understanding. Mr Warner occasionally acknowledges the problem that he presents the audience with by incorporating explanations into the text. This is particularly notable in *KT*, where the action takes place within the human brain: 'Chalone is the stopping agent that prevents the brain growing too large for its skull, as bone grows at a different rate' (1.2.10); 'Kuru. That's an unusual name, dear. Isn't it a spreading disease caused by eating live brains?' (1.6.17); 'When Quark and anti-Quark meet they annihilate

each other and emit energy. We are a family of elementary par-
ticles' (*ibid.*).

Though cleverly incorporated into dialogue and situation,
there is an element of contrivance in these glosses which is
symptomatic of a problem inherent in Mr Warner's technique.
He requires much abstruse lexical and scientific knowledge from
his audience—if he does not *expect* it then he is taking unfair
advantage of his position as author, surrounded by dictionaries,
reference books, and obliging colleagues,[2] in contrast with their
position in the theatre, thrown back on their own experience and
knowledge. The theatre-goer untrained in any branch of science
is unlikely to know that the *epigyne* (*LF*) is the external genital
plate in spiders, that a *quark* (*KT*) is a hypothetical particle
postulated to be the basic constituent of many of the so-called
elementary particles, named from Joyce's *Finnegans Wake* 'Three
quarks for Muster Mark!',[3] and that it is also the name of a
heron-like bird in the Falkland Islands:[4] neither is he likely to
be aware that *wrasse* (*ME*) is the name given to a 'thick-lipped
strong-toothed bright-coloured rock-haunting sea-fish of family
Labridae',[5] especially the 'oldwife'; the number of people
acquainted with the fact that *Shango* (*ME*) is the Yoruba god
of thunder and fertility must be strictly limited, and not even
lexicographers have at their fingertips the knowledge that a
xyster is an instrument for scraping bones, recorded in *OED* only
in 1688!

In the dialogue the vocabulary is generally not difficult,
despite scatterings of technical and scientific terms. That these
are frequently introduced merely as a matter of linguistic con-
trivance is suggested by the fact that the text usually contains

[2] Future historians of Francis Warner's poetry should have at hand a list
of his colleagues at St Peter's College, Oxford, at the relevant periods: the
Fellows of Physics (Dr G. K. Woodgate) and Biochemistry (Dr P. C. Newell)
are among those whose *obiter dicta* at the meal table or in the Senior Common
Room drew the dramatist's eye to the usual significance of the technical and
scientific terms that are dispersed throughout the plays. I (R. W. B.) chanced
on *epigyne* myself in the course of the preparation of Volume I (A–G) of
A Supplement to the O.E.D.

[3] Letter to *The Scientific American*, July 1968, p. 8.

[4] Letter to *The Times*, 28 February 1968.

[5] The somewhat Hopkinsian definition in the *Concise Oxford Dictionary*
(ed. 6, 1976).

some assistance with their meaning: 'Remember the delirious way you would fumble with the bedclothes? Carphology, you used to call it' (*LF*, 4.40); 'We're dichogamous. Self-fertilization is impossible' (*KT*, 1.9.27); 'His eyes are serpiginous, creeping from one part to the other' (*KT*, 1.9.26). Such words do not give the impression of having been acquired in a natural language-learning situation, and their contexts have an uneasy air of having been pummelled into submission to accommodate the alien item. Is it important at the particular point in the play to be told that 'in the best wife-swapping circles' a child of a two-women-one-man threesome is called 'a daisy-chain sandwich' (*M:E*, 12)? Similarly, there is nothing remarkable in the slangy style of the soldiers in *KT*, with their talk of Tommy and Jerry and Brens. The more esoteric lexical material finds no integral place in the speech of the soldiers, but has to be presented as a list (*KT*, 2.6.46). This characteristic interest in words for their own sake leads to the revival of a number of obsolete words. *Bankrupture* (*M:L*, 43) and *meretrician* (*ME*, 1.2.3) are not obscure in their context, but there seems less justification for the resuscitation of *predy*, a nautical expression recorded only twice by *OED* in the first part of the seventeenth century, since it has to be explained (*KT*, 2.7.47).

Word-coinages are not numerous, and methods of word-formation are usually straightforward, nouns used as verbs, as *strait-jacket* (*KT*, 2.7.52), *tabletop* (*ME*, 1.2.3), addition of regular affixes, as *erotoravenous* (*LF*, 3.17), *raised eyebrowish* (*KT*, 1.6.17), *self-unconsciousness* (*KT*, 1.9.29). *Mozartfully* (*KT*, 2.3.40) is of course a pun on Mozart and most artfully.

The pun is in fact the most striking and pervasive linguistic device in the plays—to list examples would involve reproduction of virtually the complete text. Human relationships are presented as involving elaborate word-games, and the punning dialogues frequently contrast with the 'poetic' and often moving monologues. The existence of double or multiple meanings keeps before the mind the awareness of human deception, of the complexity of human life, and frequently specifically the sexual motivation behind the simplest act. At its best the pun acts as a means of exposure: the title *Lying Figures* follows Shakespeare's 'Therefore I lie with her, and she with me' (Sonnet 138) in equating the sexual act with deception, and this is continued throughout the play. The pun can reveal the ambiguity in outward appearances—is Quark active or passive in 'I spend hours in the bathroom, reflecting in a mirror' (*KT*, 1.9.29)? It can condense a number of observations most effectively, as in 'In the theatre of war a soldier must take life as it comes' (*KT*, 1.1), where just existing and killing become one, or in the title itself, which equates making the time pass with slaughter. The audience is also made more aware of the meaning of words by the revival of dead metaphors and by the acquisition of an extra dimension from context. This is a particularly common technique in *LF*, where the mortuary setting gives a new significance to such expressions as 'dying for', 'vital', 'grave', or 'skeleton staff'. But it must be said that the continual punning becomes wearing. Words are wrung dry of semantic and phonological connections (for example, at *ME*, 1.5.22—for two-thirds of the page). They are introduced apparently merely in order that a pun can be made ('The French au-pair, Avocado', *ME*, 2.2.38), and similes and metaphors are invented for the same purpose ('Listening to you is like stroking a conger eel: never know when you are going to be shocked', *LF*, 3.19). This, however, is more of a problem for a reader of the text than for a theatre audience, whose attention is too occupied by the situation or the décor to allow time for every wince.

Closely connected with the pun is the juxtaposition of words of similar sound, and frequently of similar derivation, for example, 'You are alluding to an illusion' (*M:L*, 41), 'As dispensers we're indispensable' (*LF*, 2.11), 'Sympathy is innocence . . . No. Sympathy is impotence' (*KT*, 2.9.67), 'Is eschatology scatological?' (*LF*, 1.5). Both devices are part of a wider concern with the connection between things and with meanings. The plays are full of attempts at definition, many of them reductive and employing words such as 'only' or 'just': 'Marriage is the art of the impossible' (*LF*, 2.9); 'Weakness is only the reverse side of human potential' (*KT*, 1.5.13); 'Practice is only theoretical routine imposed by habit' (*KT*, 1.6.18); 'That's what love is: the shutter that comes down to prevent you thinking' (*KT*, 2.9.68); 'Democracy is only the name any modern ruling class gives to the status quo' (*ME*, 1.7.27).

Besides examining the meaning of common concepts, we are also made to look deeper into clichés and stock phrases, and thereby into social conventions. *LF*, for example, involves an almost complete reversal of expected social situations. The action involves corpses, and most activity takes place at night. The idea of the desirable is therefore not shared by the audience: 'Are you cold enough in your fridge?' asks Sapphira solicitously (1.3). And beneath it all is buried the metaphor of marriage as death for the individual: 'Mine was a white funeral' (1.2), etc.

There are a number of other related techniques in this strategy to make us question the nature—and indeed the desirability—of what is usually accepted:

1. Complete reversal of the elements of a well-known phrase or expression, for example, 'Darken our lightness' (*M:L*, 49); 'I always wanted to be a bridesmaid; and I'm only a bride' (*LF*, 3.24); 'Go where you're looking' (*KT*, 1.6.20); 'Your understanding passes all peace' (*KT*, 2.3.40).

2. Substitution of an opposite, for example, 'Let us sing a requiem for the living!' (*LF*, 1.4); 'We come from the same foreground' (*LF*, 3.35); 'You really must get a hold on unreality' (*ME*, 1.2.7); 'Don't tell me you have an immoral objection to her?' (*ME*, 1.5.20).

3. Substitution of a similar-sounding word, for example, 'There's many a true word broken in jest' (*LF*, 3.30); 'I drift from pillow to postbox' (*ME*, 1.2.7); 'If you persist in adding incest to injury' (*ME*, 2.2.37).

4. Other substitutions of unexpected lexical items, for example, 'Peace on earth, goodwill towards your husband' (*LF*, 3.16); 'What's an atrocity between friends?' (*KT*, 1.1.5).

One of the intentions of all these linguistic devices is to make the audience pay attention to every word. Exposition, particularly of medical and anatomical details (for example, in *KT* of the structure of the brain or of the chromosomal make-up of male and female), and allusion also require observation and concentration. Biblical allusions are widespread, as are echoes of Shakespeare, and one of the most poignant moments in *Lumen* is a direct quotation from James Shirley's *The Contention of Ajax and Ulysses*, 'Only the actions of the just / Smell sweet, and blossom in their dust.'

The most impressive feature of Mr Warner's language, in both poems and plays, is undoubtedly its range, from the colloquial to the abstruse, from the sensory and musical to the harsh and conceptual, or from the superficially entertaining to the deeply moving. If there is one danger, it may be that he will become merely virtuosic with language (not that this is necessarily a vice, but that Mr Warner has shown that he has more to say than mere pyrotechnics would serve), or perhaps that he will construct works of art around words instead of using words for his art. This tendency is more prevalent in the plays than the poems, and there is, no doubt, much more to a play than its text; but Mr Warner clearly emphasizes his words to his audience, and they may pay attention and yet not be entirely satisfied. This risk is avoidable if the verbal felicity of the poems is in the future more nearly matched in the plays.

2

Harold Hobson

The Warner Requiem

The first of Francis Warner's plays which I saw was *Maquettes*, a trilogy of three short dramas entitled *Emblems*, *Troat*, and *Lumen*. I was at once struck by the plays' visual and esoteric verbal mastery, their ambition to achieve difficult things, and their success in doing so. Since Mr Warner is a don at St Peter's College, it was fitting that I should have encountered *Maquettes* at the Oxford Playhouse. This was in July, 1970.

Since then Warner has written another trilogy, this time of full-length plays. These are *Lying Figures* (1971), *Killing Time* (1975), and *Meeting Ends*. *Meeting Ends* was played before *Killing Time*, since it reached the stage in 1973. Nevertheless it forms the last part of a trilogy, *Requiem*, which begins with *Lying Figures* and is brought to completion by its centre-piece *Killing Time*. This trilogy I saw, not at Oxford, but at various Edinburgh Festivals.

The Edinburgh Festival in the thirty years of its existence has been more important in the history and development of the modern theatre than many critics are willing to admit. In the mainstream drama it introduced to Britain both the Renaud–Barrault and the Jean Vilar companies: the first with a dashing and thoughtful 'Hamlet', and the second with a production of 'Richard II' that created a very deep impression. On an almost bare stage it showed Richard isolated in a pool of light, and then vanishing into surrounding darkness. Its strong visual power links it with Warner's own dramas, for the author of *Requiem* is a master of pictorial appeal touched with an edge of poetic trenchancy and sensationalism that mark him out as the most remarkable of those dramatists of our time who have striven to push the limits of theatre beyond their age-old limits, and to make artistic, philosophic, and provocative use of those freedoms of presentation which have resulted from the abolition of stage censorship and the almost total destruction of moralistic bondage.

If the first thing that impresses one about Warner's plays is the verbal intricacy and originality of their use of classical, religious, and physiological language, the second is their creative employment of female nakedness. Sometimes this is intentionally grotesque, sometimes actually terrifying, particularly so in *Lying Figures*, the first play in the trilogy. In this play one of the characters, a young girl called Xyster, admirably and indeed courageously taken by Nova Llewellyn, is involved in a scene with a cut-throat razor that is extremely important in the development of Warner's dramatic philosophy, as well as being very frightening to the audience. Mr Warner's terrible foreword to *Lying Figures* is that lethal verse from Genesis in which the Lord threatens in his anger, 'And I will wipe off the face of the earth every living thing that I have made'. It is difficult to believe that our stage will ever be able to offer to us a pictorial demonstration of this blighting of humanity more startling and more impressive, and it must be admitted more exciting, than this scene, in which Miss Llewellyn, strung upside down on the stage, is inhumanly assaulted by her companions, Gonad (Jeremy Treglown) and Epigyne (Katharine Schofield). Mr Warner has been fortunate in that his stripped actresses, chiefly Miss Schofield, Miss Llewellyn, and Josephine McNamara, are very good-looking. It is significant that in spite of this Warner has rarely or never used nudity, as for example did the artists of the Renaissance, to illustrate the loveliness of the unclothed body. In the fierceness of his attitude he resembles Swift more than Botticelli.

This is certainly not because his work is either indifferent or hostile to the satisfactions of male and female congress. These are not, in the totality of his achievement, things past reason longed for and past reason hated. The ideal towards which his plays are striving is shown clearly and beautifully in his entrancingly lyrical *Lucca Quartet*. Whether inspired by love or Italy, or by love in Italy, Francis Warner is a lyric poet of engaging charm. The keynote of the poems in *Lucca Quartet* is rest, repose, quiet happiness. There is here neither the turmoil of sexual torment, nor anything remotely resembling *post coitum triste*. A little doubt, perhaps? Yes, but not a ravaging doubt.

Does she love, was she happy, wandering the world as ours?

Children, sunshine is brief in a lifetime of showers.
Our magic carpet was perfectest joy Fate can weave—
If now unravelled, little ones, we must not grieve.

All fears and oppositions are defied.

When envy creeps up through our doors and shutters
Damning our sins, preaching anathemata
In hate of spring's cantata
Laughingly lived and sung past sneers and mutters,
Let us ignore caution's catastrophe
And breed proud children in shared ecstasy.

Love is in fact an idyll.

Peace in the afternoon
   Sparkling eyes;
Sunbeams are rafters
   Stillness flies:
Wildwood contentment
   On hillside and path
Pinetree and olive
   Watch the hearth.

Farmyards of Tuscany
   Cupped in hills
Move in the shadows that
   Brightness fills.
Steep paths hesitate
   Stepping in green;
Dark wine for cover
   And lover's screen . . .

May wings stretch over you
   Spring touch your vein
Loveliness lighten
   To childhood again
Falling hair fasten
   Love to your breast
By Florentine scentfall
   Caressed.

The setting of the *Lucca Quartet* poems is a perfectly natural
Florentine landscape and farmhouse. There is a chess-set, and
'sultry postcards',

> ... Carracci's Bacchante
> In tongue-tied exultation
> And the Urbino Venus caught in languor,

and there is Mother too, 'shocked stiff', perhaps understandably
so. All these are completely materialistically real, solid things,
such as it would cause us no surprise to encounter ourselves.

Lying Figures also, at any rate at the start, has a realistic
setting. It opens in a mortuary. Gonad wheels on a couple of
corpses, an old man and an old woman (Sapphira and Laz)
and puts them into a couple of refrigerators. Before doing this
(he is smoking) he pinches open the mouth of one of the
corpses, and taps his cigarette ash into it, for Mr Warner stands
no more in awe of death than of the beauty of the female body.
Both are to him instruments of pictorial and philosophical
poetry.

If this is realism it is a gruesome realism far from the lyric
happiness of *Lucca Quartet*. And it is a realism soon left behind,
for a dazzling display of surrealism immediately takes its place,
which continues throughout the whole drama. The refrigerator
doors open, and the dead Laz and Sapphira begin to talk in a
manner which shows that they are not unacquainted with
Samuel Beckett. 'We are born in excrement', says Laz happily,
'and even so we decompose.' Sapphira replies with one of Mr
Warner's famously sordid similes: 'Like used soap in an un-
cleaned-out hotel'. Mr Warner is highly skilled in the kind of
metaphor that in a single sentence gives the atmosphere of a
Graham Greene novel.

Not, however, that his imagination does not soar and explore,
rather like Pater's Mona Lisa. Gonad's unfaithful wife Epigyne
is having an affair with his employer, Guppy, who is given to
considerable flights of fancy. 'To voyage across the seas!' he
exclaims, and then with extravagant gestures continues, 'Seek
out the burial customs of the Incas. Investigate the pyramids,
annotate the catacombs, gather fossils, resurrect dinosaurs,
excavate mounds, relive the Coliseum! Burn with Rome, flame
with Troy, drown with Sodom, get stoned with Gomorrah, find

souvenirs from Paschendaele, hear the Last Post bugled through the Menin Gate, and return in time to visit the tomb of the Unknown Warrior in St Paul's'—a burst of eloquence to which the exasperated Epigyne, pleased neither with marriage nor with adultery, replies, 'Holy God!'

Epigyne begins the second act of the play, dressed as a bride, in a black wedding-dress with a black bouquet. She enters the stage in a very stately way, and curtsies to the audience. She then bends her head in prayer, and launches into a long speech about marriage (Gonad 'sleeps like a furnace') and the interminable time that Guppy takes to come over to their bungalow after Gonad has left for his night work at the mortuary. Marriage is in fact, in the desperate outlook of *Lying Figures*, a sham, even a black sham, a fact symbolically illustrated when Epigyne turns round to go upstage. For the bridal dress is not a complete bridal dress. 'The audience', says Warner, 'suddenly see that she is naked from head to heel, as the bridal dress has no back to it'. Epigyne was played by Katharine Schofield with a timing and an aplomb which gave to this scene a very startling quality.

In the circumstances it is not surprising that, when Gonad breaks into poetry, his verse has little of Lucca about it. He cries:

> The wrench of birth. Two bodies, puffed marshmallows
> Pressed into crying, still slimed from the womb.
> A sky shrunk to a pillow wet with grief,
> An earth contracted to a spasmed room ...

> Let me reach out across the darkening lake!
> Oh little children, yet the briefest while
> We live to grieve our bearers, till the rake
> Claws out our wisdom with our bloody tears.

It will by now have struck the reader—though no critic of the play in performance seemed to notice it—that the names of the characters are rather odd. Guppy may be familiar enough, because it has a sort of Dickensian ring about it. It might have belonged to an absurd young man in 'Great Expectations'. But there is nothing familiar about Gonad and Epigyne, nor about Xyster, who is just about to enter: not unless you are at home with botany and surgery. These terms are evidence of Warner's esoteric learning. Epigyne is formed from a term of which Vine's 'Sach's Botany' says (1882) that 'the flower finally is epigynous when it possesses an actually inferior ovary'. Gonad, like his wife, is also defective, for a gonad is 'an undifferentiated germ-gland serving both as ovary and spermery'. Xyster, however, is more formidable, for a xyster is an instrument for scraping bones. The *Oxford English Dictionary*, after an allusion to Blancard's *Physiological Dictionary* of 1684, gives one quotation, from Holme, who in 1688 speaks of it in his *Armoury* with some distaste as an instrument for shaving and scraping filthy bones.

But it is Xyster who is mutilated, in a scene to which I have already referred. To show that I have not exaggerated it is worth while to quote Warner's own stage directions at this point in the play.

> Xyster, centre-stage, raises arms and takes off dress—her sole article of clothing—in one movement. She lies face downwards on stage, the crown of her head midstage, soles of feet upstage centre. Gonad and Epigyne fasten the two soft straps, which are the ends of the hanging ropes, one to each ankle. Once fastened, she is hoisted upside-down by the ankles to hang like a starfish, her back to the audience, her front reflected in the mirrors, her long hair spilling down to brush the floor.

> EPIGYNE: The razor.
> GONAD: (*To* EPIGYNE, *gently*) Anything more is inhuman.
> EPIGYNE: (*Handing him an open cut-throat razor*) Prove your manhood, my tender love.

> Gonad raises cut-throat razor, and as he brings it down between her legs the lights black, and off stage is heard the sound of a sheet being torn. No scream.

Nova Llewellyn played this terrifying, and indeed dangerous scene, with commendable courage, but instead of spreading her legs wide like a starfish, she kept them together. This was no doubt to avoid accidents, but it may be the reason that later Warner insisted that his text should be followed to the letter.

It will be noticed that in this horrifying scene some kind of tenderness makes a brief if ineffective appearance, and this note of tenderness is again struck at the end of the play. Another corpse comes into the mortuary. This time it is the skeleton of a child, and Gonad leans over it tenderly, his face lit by a candle. He pauses, and then speaks the final words: 'I had hoped so much for you.' There is another pause, and then he adds, 'Emptiness enfolds. Darkness encroaches on the light, and in lightness we dare not comprehend.'

It may be taken by analogy and nomenclature that in *Lying Figures*, the Fall of Man, and that which first brought death into the world and all our woe, encompasses not only men and women that move, but also botanic life that does not. In the second part of the trilogy, *Killing Time*, Warner seems to extend this damnation from men and sex and plants to war and the life of rivers and the ocean. One of the characters, a soldier at war, facing another with fixed bayonet, is called Squaloid, a word to which Buckland in 1836 had this reference: 'The third family of Squaloids, or true sharks, commences with the crustaceous formation.' Another, Quark (Andee Cromarty), is suggestive of the croaking of spring frogs in a pool. In the third play, *Meeting Ends*, Katharine Schofield plays Wrasse, of whom it has been formidably written: 'One or other species belonging to the acanthopterygian family Labridae, or especially the genus Labrus of bony, thick-lipped, marine fishes.' Nothing, it seems, can escape, no single living thing.

Killing Time is concerned with the mind as well as the body of man, and it finds this mind rotten. It begins with a long and impressive, but powerfully pessimistic speech, on the nature of Fallen Man.

When two dogs fight and one of them can grip no longer, he rolls over and offers his throat, and the other turns away. It's a natural instinct that prevents all dogs fighting to the death. Even wolves have a code for killing their kind. But man and the fox are deformed. . . . The fox kills far beyond his need for food, for pleasure, until exhausted. And the human baby is anonymous until his teeth grow. Then the shape of the jaw gives the parents' likeness. He can bite. There is no innocence save lack of experience; and man, being a questing creature, cannot accept life on those terms, so war is a fever in our brain.

Then there is a trenches scene, and after that a crucial lecture given by Chalone, 'pompous and fussy, wearing half-cut glasses, full-bottomed wig and codpiece, black gown open down the front'.

This speech, which is very long, is vital to *Killing Time* in that it tackles the murderous propensities of man literally head and front. The head, or rather the inside of the head, is there for the audience to see, and Warner goes to extreme lengths so that the audience should see it properly. Chalone lectures the audience holding a pointer 'with which he gestures at the large photograph of the brain he has before him'. Warner emphasizes the importance of Chalone's speech by indicating precisely which these photographs should be. They are: DeArmond, Fusco, and Dewey, 'Structure of the Human Brain, A Photographic Atlas', Oxford University Press, 1974. Page five, lateral surface as photograph 1; page nine, medial surface as 2; cover photograph as 3; page 3, superior surface as 4.

The lecture itself is of sufficient importance to be quoted in full.

CHALONE: (*Pointing to photograph 1*). There's something wrong with this. Nature went astray. This is the cerebellum, at the back of the skull behind the brain stem, and under the great hemispheres of the cerebrum. Cerebellum means 'little brain'. If the cerebellum (*Pointing to photograph 2*) is split down the middle, the folds form a pattern which resembles a tree. This has been called from time immemorial the tree of life. (*Pointing to photograph 3.*) Unfortunately, it is also the tree of death.

We know the wiring circuits of the eyes, the olfactory organs, and the sexual. More generally, the reticular formation of the brain on the main brain stem keeps you aroused (*Pointing to a member of the audience*) and awake! We know the senses of arousal. We know the seven nerves of the cortex. First, climbing fibres for comedy; second, mossy fibres for tragedy. As tragedy is the higher mode, the mossy fibres stimulate the largest number of cells and provoke negative feedback. Comedy on the other hand reasserts balance and peace, so the climbing fibres spring naturally from the two inferior olives of the brain stem. Third, fourth, fifth, and

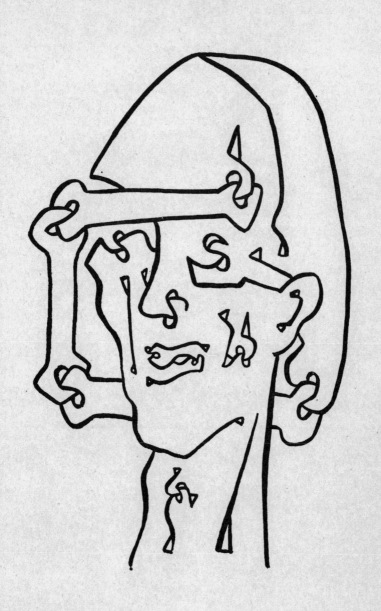

sixth, the indigenous ones, each with their own character-
istics, and running to and fro among each other—basket,
granule, Golgi, and stellate. And finally, an overall judge,
with checks and balances, serving as sole master of the
system, (*with modest pride*) Purkinje . . .

The left hemisphere reacts to visual input with verbal
response, and the right hemisphere to tactual responses. The
left hemisphere, for example, cannot draw a square. No.

Chalone then continues his speech until at the very end, after
all the carnages we have seen, the irrationality of the universe,
and the perverseness of men, women, and children, and the
ludicrous excesses into which the passion of sex leads them, we
arrive at one slender hope, a hope that is not explained until the
last pages of the final play, *Meeting Ends*, in which Mithraism
supplants Christianity, but does not bring the hope hoped for.

These then are Chalone's vital sentences.

It would be a miracle were it not for one basic fact. The only
moral direction of the entire unit is towards survival. This it
has, of course, in common with animals. What distinguishes
man from animals is not speech, writing, and such, for which
there are many analogues, but his ability to commit suicide.
Even lemmings don't do this intentionally. They swim madly,
hoping to get to the other side. (*Pause.*) But you can argue
that this ability of man also implies its opposite, and that—
may—save us from the holocaust. On the answer to this
question hangs the future of the world. Goodnight.

Suicide has been mentioned, and suicide of an extremely
bizarre visual impact we are then given. There is a table in the
shape of a human brain, and over it hangs the figure of a nude
woman, except that her neck and part of her back are hidden
by a large silver wedding-bell which covers the harness by
which she is suspended. This woman is played by Evie Garratt,
who has given many fine performances in Warner's plays,
and is somewhat more mature than her fellow-players, who are
all in the first flush of youth. Her age adds a new dimen-
sion to Warner's areas of destruction, as she swings to and fro
like a clapper in a bell, her bare bottom always towards the
audience.

This is an essential part of Warner's stagecraft in his use of nudity as a moral force. Though Mother may be shocked ever so stiff, and Aunt Edna have to be removed from the theatre foaming at the mouth; though his mastery of unusual learning is very striking, his power to make puns and jokes apparently illimitable, and his capacity for bizarre vision unrivalled, Warner's unique achievement, at which not even Ionesco has succeeded, is to exhibit the naked body as always associated with danger, absurdity, terror, or humiliation. Katharine Schofield in a wedding-dress that reveals her stark nude from head to heel at the back, and again in a telephone kiosk; Nova Llewellyn savagely mutilated with Jeremy Treglown's cut-throat razor; Andee Cromarty made to lie unclothed under the knife of the guillotine; Josephine McNamara sitting on a chamber-pot, and then, finding herself unable to make water, playing the first two bars of 'Abide with me' on a harmonium; and, most important of all, Evie Garratt's swaying nude bottom—this is what Mr Warner thinks of the flesh.

But at the beginning of *Meeting Ends* he says: 'Yet in my flesh shall I see God.' Yet this too is by mutilation of the body, for Ensoff (Martin Scott), a ceremonial figure, speaks the final triumphant poem of the play only after he has been castrated.

> The silent stars play havoc with our toys
> But we have kingdoms that they cannot touch.

This is the hope that Chalone spoke of. The total ruin and scorn of the flesh, seen sensationally through these astounding plays, is the alternative way to that peace and bliss found by another, quieter road in *Lucca Quartet*.

3

David Self

The Requiem: A Surrealist Script

As Harold Hobson wrote in *The Sunday Times* (28.iv.74), 'Most people will see that in *Meeting Ends* there is a lot of nudity.' He might have made the observation with equal validity about any of the three plays which form *Requiem*. It is a trilogy which has a number of erotic moments, and certainly many people might not see beyond these moments: the plays (and even the published texts) *are* visually exciting and *do* have an immediate and obvious impact. Because of this, it is possible in any serious consideration of *Requiem* to concentrate on the tautly complex prose and verse and to scorn the visual as being either just a sop to the groundlings, an entertainment to lighten an academic text, or possibly as being the self-indulgent fantasizing of an intellectual. A critic might also disdain to analyse what has such an immediate appeal for fear of appearing ponderous or even ridiculous.

However, the visual element of *Requiem* is an integral part of its overall design (I use the word with all its theatrical connotations) and its design is in no way casual. Francis Warner's stage directions are always precise, part of a total concept and never simply decoration. For example, in *Lying Figures* (Act Two) Xyster enters 'and then stands absolutely still in position, facing front, her right wrist horizontally across her navel, her left down by her side, palm of hand flat against thigh'. These are the directions of a playwright who is very concerned with exactly how his plays are to be staged. 'Throughout the *Requiem*, where photographs differ from text, the text should be followed', says a note in the front of the texts. Warner is an artist who paints precise stage pictures: he is not an academic writer who leaves the business of staging plays to others.

Because the visual is such an important part of the plays (whether the visual be erotic or not) it is proper that its nature should be considered in any survey of the *Requiem*. In this short essay, I do not intend to gloss each image—that may be done by a future editor of the texts. What I hope to do is to offer some sort of rationale to directors and designers that may help them to see a philosophy that lies above and behind the individual scenes, and that dictates a specific approach and style.

*   *   *

Shakespeare's theatre understood symbolism. Beneath the stage was hell, the wooden planking on which the actors strutted was the earth, and above there stretched the canopy of the heavens. Anyone who wore riding-boots was a messenger and the moment a chair was brought on stage we were indoors.

The development of the proscenium arch resulted in naturalism. Gradually the stage became crowded with detail as (to paraphrase Hazlitt) the theatre became the triumph of scene-shifters, scene-painters, machinists and dress-makers, and manufacturers of moon and stars.

This century we have seen first the cinema and then television appropriate both naturalism and realism, and (perhaps in self-defence rather than for more positive reasons) theatre directors and designers gave up the battle to compete with the epics of the wide screen and the social realism of television. Rather, they embraced a sort of impressionism. Even realistic drama (for example, *Look Back in Anger* and some of Wesker's plays) relied on cut-away scenery, flown structures, and directional lighting which suggested rather than created location. (Incidentally, but importantly, such impressionistic staging did also allow the creation of atmosphere and mood in a way that had hardly been attempted before in the theatre.) Such a style was also dominant at Stratford in the sixties when the Shakespearean canon was successfully worked in a black box with properties, elaborate lighting, special effects, and (most of all) costume, replacing scenery.

Superficially Francis Warner's plays appear to owe a lot to this impressionistic style: the black background, the striking props (such as the sides of meat in *Maquettes*, the guillotine in *Killing Time*, and the mousetrap in *Meeting Ends*), and stunning costumes (or equally stunning nudity) all seem to be part of this style.

In fact, Warner's plays are not impressionistic in conception: they are as sharply focused as a photograph, and have the foreground clarity of a dream. We are told that *Emblems* (the first of the *Maquettes*) deliberately sets out to explore its themes in the style of a surrealist painting: many critics have pointed out the surrealism in (at least) *Lying Figures*. It is my contention that in fact the whole of the major trilogy is surrealistic and so positively so that this must be the guiding factor when realizing it on stage.

Surrealism explores fearlessly man's fate and destiny. It seeks to understand the visible, tangible world and also an inner reality. It is a concept that embodies politics and morality, and which exalts freedom. 'What was special to Surrealism was its determination to lay bare the deepest hidden cogs of human behaviour, and link both literary and artistic expression with a new-articulated "psychology of the depths".'[1] This is the matter and the concern of Warner in these three poetic and intensely visual plays. It was through poetry that Surrealism first revealed its nature, but for many it is in the visual arts that its manifestations are most obvious, and it is its visual manifestations with which we are now concerned.

Warner's *Requiem* draws heavily on surrealist paintings. Just as the prose and verse are filled with literary puns, with classical and contemporary half-quotes, so too is the action filled with parodies of, and quotations from, the work of many painters— particularly the work of Paul Delvaux.

Delvaux was never formally associated with the Parisian circle of surrealist artists, but his works (typical of which are *The Hands* and *Venus Asleep*) conform to the Breton formula of surrealism: 'Surrealism rests on belief in the superior reality of certain forms of association hitherto neglected, on the omnipotence of the dream, on the disinterested play of thought.'[2] In his paintings, sharply delineated nudes walk unself-consciously through geometrical streets of fully dressed people where the skeleton of death is often literally present. His is the liberated world of Freud where our dreams are as real as reality and usually more telling.

[1] Waldberg, Patrick (1970), *The Initiators of Surrealism*.
[2] Breton, André (1924), *Manifeste du Surréalisme*, translated by David Gascoyne.

Whoever would appreciate the intricacies of the *Requiem* would do well to study the work of Delvaux and others. Whoever would direct the plays would also do well to attempt to capture the dream-like movements of Delvaux's stately, composed, placid figures—and also (paradoxically) seek to preserve the spontaneity and fluidity of dreams. 'The disinterested play of thought' moves fast. Just as it would kill the texts to play them slowly, allowing every member of the audience time to ponder over each allusion, so too would it kill the plays if the staging were so ponderous that we had time to detach ourselves between each scene and question logically and objectively the images we had just seen. Ideally we should leap cinematically from one scene to another; images and properties should materialize as from the subconscious. We should not be allowed to wonder how the trick has been achieved theatrically: it should happen with apparent spontaneity—which places considerable demands upon the designer and especially upon the stage manager. Indeed for the plays to be produced satisfactorily they demand an extremely well-equipped stage and perhaps also call for such electronic devices as back projection (especially in the case of *Killing Time*; see below).

In writing the plays, Warner has borrowed much from the grammar of television, and particularly from a special style of studio production. It is a style that has been little used in television drama but is common in current affairs programmes and in studio based documentaries. Rather than build an elaborate and fairly meaningless studio set, the television director places the 'discussion' or television essay 'in limbo'—that is, the presenter and other participants are televised against blacks; and salient maps, diagrams, and properties (the latter often dramatically lit) are superimposed on the picture—either behind or to one side of the person in shot. Without the clutter or distraction of a set, but with the support of well-chosen three-dimensional properties and illustrations, and in the glare of precisely directed white light, the arguments are developed.

This is in fact a style that admirably suits (especially) *Lying Figures* and *Meeting Ends*. In *Lying Figures* it is enough that (as in the Elizabethan style) the bare stage represents the earth, and against the blackness of chaos or limbo are superimposed the characters and the properties that make the author's points.

Note that—to make these points—the properties (such as refrigerators, the owl-mask, the tree) must be realistic as we would expect in a television essay and not simply impressionistic as we might accept in some drama. As in a television documentary, as in a surrealist painting, if we are to see a telephone box (as we do in *Meeting Ends*) then we must believe that we see a real one. Television style demands realistic properties; so too does surrealistic painting, where an effect is achieved by the juxtaposition of the realistic with the unexpected. Dali's watches are horrific because they are so real. The stage designer and manager must not be content with symbolic props in surrealist drama. It is after all distracting and confusing if we adopt a syntax of one language (note Warner's use of television terms in stage directions such as the 'Fade to black' at the end of Act One of *Lying Figures*) but then use the vocabulary of another. So the stage properties must be sufficiently real to suit the style of television (and also to produce the shock-incongruity of a surrealist work of art) but yet clean enough in line to make their points sharply and concisely. Admirably successful in achieving this was the original production in Edinburgh in 1973 of *Meeting Ends*.

From the moment we heard the opening drums, the last post, and Ensoff's declamation from limbo (a detached, superimposed chancellor of the mind), our imaginations were assaulted and engaged. Then, in rapid succession came a fast-flowing stream of surrealist images from the subconscious—the pilloried women; Shango, the bull-headed predator; and, later, comes the cinematic split-screen technique of the telephone-box scene, economically establishing distance, relationship, and frustration. Later images are equally telling—the brightly painted baby gypsy caravan, Shango's wheel, and the disturbing realism of the bath—isolated in a mental void. If *Meeting Ends* can be (and was) produced in a way that matches its writing, *Killing Time* presents more problems.

Unlike the other two plays (which are set, Elizabethan style, on a plain stage that represents the earth, and which, dreamlike, can instantaneously become a localized scene) *Killing Time* is set firmly in the human brain, and as we are only gradually to appreciate this fact, this calls for back-projection techniques or special lighting that can gradually sketch in or illuminate realistic scenery. Within this overall setting, we must also believe in *places* such as the brain-within-the-brain of Act One, scene five; and the urban foxhole of Act Two. Again, these must be sufficiently realistic as to be surrealist—and even if this proves within the capabilities of designer and stage carpenter, it presents the stage manager with enormous problems on a small stage. *Killing Time* met considerable difficulty in Edinburgh, where the problem of setting up scenes on the small Jordanburn Theatre stage robbed many of them of their potential impact, as well as producing uncomfortable noises from back stage.

To some, this might seem trivial. I would disagree. *Killing Time* is a series of vignettes on the subject of war, carefully counterpointed to reflect the working patterns of the brain. The brain works fast. So must the play.

So indeed must the whole trilogy.

*   *   *

In a period when the director reigns supreme in the theatre, Shakespeare has obvious attractions. Such is his writing that his plays will work in a number of interpretations, and a director may produce a given play as either a realistic domestic tragedy or as an impressionistic epic with equal chances of success. But the work of others, Pinter for example, does not permit such a variety of interpretation—the author has dictated even the size of the pauses, never mind the scale of the play; and it is my contention that (despite possible appearances to the contrary) Francis Warner's plays (like Samuel Beckett's) are as tightly written and as restricting on the director's imagination as are Pinter's.

This is no bad thing. But it must not be forgotten. The plays are surrealist and must be produced on that assumption, which has both technical and interpretative implications. The stage directions and properties must be followed exactly and with an appreciation of the quality of surrealist art; and the political and moral observations interpreted within the terms of surrealist philosophy. 'Surrealism . . . represents the most recent romantic attempt to break with "things as they are" in order to replace them by others, in full activity, in process of birth, whose mobile contours are inscribed in filigree in the heart of existence.'[3]

[3] Raymond, Marcel (1950), *From Baudelaire to Surrealism.*

Such a general statement will serve as a guide to the *Requiem*. The trilogy may appear complex and daunting; it may appear a wonderful chance for directorial indulgence. It must, however, be produced with a lightness and delicacy that will give it speed and fluency. It must also be produced with panache and flamboyance, in order to portray the subconscious where emotions are vibrant and positive—and if this is achieved then (as a bonus) the production in question might also realize the touching moments of lyricism which can be mined from the text.

4

Melinda Camber Porter

The Use of Structure in the Plays

The structure of a work can always be deciphered or imposed by the critic. Any play, no matter how fluid, anarchic, or fragmentary can become a hunting-ground for leitmotif, pattern, and repetition. Structure need not be explicit; it may be unravelled by the intelligence or merely felt as a rhythm. It may be created by a repetition of ruptures in the text. In short, any text is ready material for structuralist analysis.

But Francis Warner's three one-act plays and three full-length plays are not only open to structuralist analysis: they necessitate it. The texts are almost brazen about their own construction. The author explicates his process of creation as he creates, like a commentator who breathlessly tries to keep up with the rapid, unforeseeable progress of a race; but Mr Warner is both the runner and the commentator.

The playwright is unwilling to camouflage or blur that which has already reached consciousness. His critical faculties hack away at the primary material, dissect intuition, leaving one with the impression that reason is an assault. That the words of intelligence are as brutal as the physical violence on stage.

Mr Warner wastes no time and makes no compromises when it comes to revealing the violence of the critical faculties. In *Killing Time* the stage lights up or the book is opened and we are told: 'The stage is a giant human brain.'

There is no suggestion. No landscape which could be associated with or become reminiscent of the human brain. The symbolic has already been explicated. Similarly, Mr Warner knows that he wishes his characters to represent parts of the human brain and, consequently, he does not bother to give them human names. In *Meeting Ends*, which, as the title suggests, is based on the themes of resolution and love, the playwright reduces the stage to a circle. There is no concession to realism. No attempt to reproduce a landscape which the playwright identified with love and resolution. The stage is a geometrical form, abstracted from the particular and the personal.

Already, one can see that the explicit structuring of the playwright is of a different nature from the critic's unravelling of patterns. The intellect does not calm the material; it exacerbates. The ruthless self-consciousness does not appease the violence of the material. It is used as another dramatic structure which intensifies the wildness and frenzy of Mr Warner's dramatic world.

Structural analysis has been used as a means of 'objectifying' criticism, a way of getting round the notion that the critic is dependent on his own personal reaction. It has been used to neutralize the critic's position. Mr Warner reverses this process, by revealing the emotional charge that is created by the conflict between the 'primary' and 'secondary' processes. But, as well as being a demystification of this recently acquired critical stance, it is also a dig at himself. Ripping the flesh from his own material, ripping the mystery from the process of creation, he puts himself on trial and refuses to accept a justification provided by a ready-made aesthetic.

Sometimes, however, one senses the fun that the playwright derives from the limitless games that the intellect can play, when divorced from facts and feelings. There is an evident joy in the enquiry into the process of creation, and an inebriating ease in the movements of the intellect. Mr Warner creates his plays as if they were living organisms; with the three one-act Maquettes, *Emblems*, *Troat*, and *Lumen*, he sows the seeds of the three full-length plays, *Lying Figures*, *Killing Time*, and *Meeting Ends*. Three embryos give birth to three fully-fledged works. But the relationship between the maquettes is not merely numerical. A heredity is created, rather as in Zola's Rougon-Maquarts saga, except that the genes are created within the fabric of the text and not simply between the characters. The major themes of Death (*Lying Figures*), War (*Killing Time*), and Love (*Meeting Ends*) are precisely foreshadowed, in a similar sequence, in the maquettes. *Emblems*, the first of the three, leaves us in no suspense concerning its theme. The first word-play is on 'mourning'.

BRIDE ONE: I'm sorry. I should have said 'Good afternoon'. It's not my day.

BRIDE TWO: It was morning.
BRIDE ONE: (*startled*) Mourning? At our wedding?

Similarly, in the first play of the trilogy, *Lying Figures*, the theme of death is stated immediately. At first, we are plunged into total darkness as we hear the sound of an ambulance. The stage lights up to reveal two mortuary refrigerators. Again, the opening word-play centres on 'deaf' and 'death'.

LAZ: Why bother? All my life I've been dying for this.
SAPPH: (*stung*) Oh. All right! It's not vital.
LAZ: (*humbled*) I'm mortified.

In *Troat*, which heralds the theme of War, and in *Killing Time*, the soldier and the heaping of coals onto the fire leads us, as do the opening word-plays, into the major theme.

YOUNG MAN: You may watch the road but you are not a sentry. There isn't a war on, you know.
OLD MAN: Several.

Lumen, with its tenderness and flickers of light struggling to survive in a black landscape, points forward to the tone of *Meeting Ends*.

> Three wise men from the west reach for the moon
> And far in space look back on the good earth
> Unlikely in vast silence to cocoon
> Life on its surface, which may be as stark
> As this dead rock of sand and crusty dearth
> Now reached . . .

This process of construction, by its perfect precision, its rigorous consistency and logic, reveals a self-consciousness which has become one of the hallmarks of so-called modernist literature. The creator is unable or unwilling to take the process of creation for granted. Valéry watches himself watching himself in an infinity of mirrors which represents the conscious faculties. The avant-garde French poet writes about writing. Painters paint their own techniques and eliminate the subject matter which had moulded their search for technique in the past.

But the new adage of Technique for Technique's Sake, or The Medium is the Message, presents particular problems for the writer and the reader. Language presupposes the notion of subject and object, of meaning as well as form. Language cannot be used as a merely sensual form of communication. The 'significant' is indivisible from the 'signifié'; there is no intuitive, natural link between the sound and the sense, except in rare instances. Magical formulae and incantations depend on a preliminary knowledge of the ideology which underlies their usage. A poem spoken in an incomprehensible language cannot have the force of a simple melody. It is not within language that pure form finds its expression.

It is not surprising that Mr Warner read music for a year at the London College of Music before going up to Cambridge on a music scholarship. His attempt to pare down to a minimum the 'referential' nature of language and to make construction a subject-matter in its own right suggests a desire to bring literature as close to music as is possible. Evidently, in most dramas, the rhythm speaks. Suspense, relief, boredom, and fear can all be communicated by the pace and placing of scenes. But Mr Warner is not content to allow this habitual musical element in drama to remain at an unspoken level. Yet again, he submits it to analysis and states its presence.

Troat, the second of the maquettes, is subtitled *A Double Fugue*: a fugue with two subjects and counter-subjects. First, the Bass enters in the form of the Old Man and the first and second themes are stated. Then the Tenor, the Young Man, takes up the two themes while the Old Man gives two counter-subjects to the themes. Similarly, the entry of the Woman provides an Alto and the Boy becomes a Treble. The interplay continues until the stretto when the voices come closer together. The climbing Treble brings them together in a violent final chord which resolves all the themes and counter-subjects for the last time. The Boy speaks his final note:

And the Lord saw Man as beautiful and imperfect . . .
Then, in a clear, unaccompanied treble voice, [the Boy] sings Nunc Dimittis to Tonus Peregrinus.

The old man drops a brazier full of red-hot coals on the heads of the young man and woman who are about to kiss and one hears a violent scream.

The words, which have acted in the playwright's mind as musical notes, suddenly reveal themselves to be just that. The boy sings. The process of the construction of a Double Fugue

breaks out into the open and is made explicit. The process of
creation is unveiled and it is by no means accidental that this
moment of revelation is almost the climax of *Troat*. But not
quite. Having sung loud the process behind his construction,
the playwright ends with a natural sound, a shriek. As in
Rimbaud's *Illuminations*, the artificial world created by words is
constructed, glorified, rendered sacred and omnipotent, and in
the final verse the artefact is destroyed and the preceding verses
are brought into question. This movement is visually described
in the prose poem 'Les Ponts':

'Un rayon blanc, tombant du haut du ciel anéantit cette
comédie.'

The 'willing suspension of disbelief' which was once an essen-
tial element in drama is destroyed, as a tool, only to be resur-
rected as a subject-matter.

In Act Three of *Lying Figures*, the form of the classical fugue
is decipherable, although it is of a more complex nature than
that to be found in *Troat*. Again, we find the Double Fugue, with
Epigyne as Alto and Gonad as Tenor. Once they have intro-
duced their subjects and counter-subjects, they are joined by a
Bass, in the form of Guppy and, finally, by the Soprano, Xyster.
This time, the climbing Treble is replaced by a descending Bass
(Guppy), who exits on a scream. But he, like the Boy in *Troat*, is
separated from the final three-part chord (Gonad, Epigyne, and
Xyster). The final note is, yet again, a natural sound:

Offstage is heard the sound of a sheet being torn. No scream.

The final stage directions are particularly revealing of Mr
Warner's method of construction. For the readers of the play,
the statement 'no scream', suggests that there should, logically,
be a scream, given the context of the preceding text and texts.
The absence of a scream is as significant as its presence because
the preceding structure should have prepared us for it.

Mr Warner works from a complicity with the audience which
is, perhaps, hopeful rather than justified. For a text which
consistently abandons the domain of intuition and feeling to
the mercy of the intellect can often find itself without its most
essential tool of attack and persuasion. For once the critical
faculties are called on, the movements of doubt, suspicion, and

disbelief are brought into play. Mr Warner makes it impossible for the audience to be carried along by any of the habitual rituals of drama. He demands of his audience a careful balancing act between the conscious and the unaware, and this is a tough request.

Mr Warner's ironic method of divesting his own powers of creation of their mystery, his wish to dissect the body he loves, demands a solitary, careful reading. He asks his audience to follow through his dismembering of a text. And though it is evident that Mr Warner finds criticism a passionate and dramatic process, he often takes for granted that the critical faculties of his audience are as virulent and passionate as his own. It is not surprising that his plays have sometimes received a sceptical response when one considers that Mr Warner has purposively evoked these very faculties in his audience.

But the emotive language and sets also evoke the simple emotions of disgust, pleasure, and excitement. The critical violence is equalled by an abundance of unconscious and uncontrolled material. Even the puns which fold mathematically in and out use techniques of association which Lacan deciphers in dreams. The sleeping and waking mind are given equivalent potency, and do battle. But rarely does Mr Warner suggest that these forces can harmonize or learn from each other. They co-exist as a conflict. The gap between the anarchic, anti-social material and the fertile area of intelligence expands to become an abyss. And it is within this no man's land where meeting is battle that the plays are created. At times, the brutality of the visual world threatens to destroy the empire of language. At times, the words take off into a gymnastic display, leaving behind the world of common sense. Each domain fights for its supremacy, but neither gains sway.

The ideal of integration is absent from Mr Warner's venture. The parts of the mind are as separate and often as incompatible as the characters in a play. The boundaries between the units are stated and the dissociation is stated as an undeniable fact rather than as a failure which may be cured.

One of the painters who has been a forceful influence on Mr Warner's work is Paul Klee, and although Bacon and Moore are of more autobiographical importance than this artist, Klee's methods seem to have penetrated into the text more forcefully.

In Douglas Hall's introduction to the 1974 Arts Council Catalogue of a Paul Klee exhibition, we find an uncanny fraternity.

The critic asks:

'How should one read these pictures? Being discontinuous, the lines cannot be read as locating any image, or organically as parts of a whole. The whole picture field is therefore alive with possibilities of relationships, none of which can claim supremacy. The notion of location has been replaced by the most acute projection of interval, which exists all over the field as a power of attraction or repulsion, eliminating any necessity for a hierarchy of importance among the drawn forms.'

And it is not only in painting that one can find parallels for Mr Warner's stance. Antonioni states that the characters in his films are as important as the objects and landscapes that surround them. There is no hierarchy—only elements which can enter into various relationships with each other.

Mr Warner does not hesitate to see his characters as musical themes; he can present a slaughter as a logical, musical, or visual element. He can shift backwards and forwards from the recognizable human dialogue to poetry. The rigorous construction becomes a circuit through which a protean charge may flow. The dramatic mask, and with it the possibility of losing shame and morality, has been extended, if not squeezed dry.

For, with the mask, the actor could lose his social persona and allow the 'primitive' self to run riot; the social mores disappeared as the face hid behind an extravagant image. Similarly, except in a more sophisticated form, the protean transformation of character into colour, shape, or melody acts as a similar mask which allows sexual and violent fantasy to appear without the censorship of a particular and familiar society.

Technique for Technique's Sake loses its aptness as an adage, as did Art for Art's Sake. Both were techniques for banishing morality and the guilt that accompanies it. Both were techniques for blinding the audience before overwhelming them with unwanted insights into unavowed worlds. As blood becomes merely a colour in a system of colour relationships, as the shriek becomes a coda, the social world is left behind. But whether these techniques can suspend the moral beliefs of an audience is a question which only time can answer.

5

Glyn Pursglove

Erected Wit and Infected Will
Some notes towards a reading of Meeting Ends

1

The earliest of Mr Warner's works which I have on my shelves is *Perennia*, his epyllion in Spenserian stanzas, first published by Raymond Lister's Golden Head Press at Cambridge in 1962. The poem bears as its epigraph the following sentences:

> Only by looking towards the Beyond as the true goal of ecstasy can man become balanced in the present. Balance depends on ecstasy.

The sentences come from Edgar Wind's remarkable book *Pagan Mysteries in the Renaissance*—a work much loved by Mr Warner. The quotation comes from Professor Wind's chapter on 'The Medal of Pico della Mirandola', part of his extended discussion of Renaissance Neoplatonism's dealings with the Three Graces.

Perennia sets up a duality which was to play an important part in the later plays. Perennia is a Psyche figure:

> And then more lovely than a well played lute
> The voice of Eros spoke beside her ear
> Telling her to go in and eat the fruit
> That lay upon the table, and to cheer
> Herself with honey-mead, the country beer;
> And tell him all that she had felt that day;
> To lie down on the bed of maiden-hair
> And spend the hours in happiness and play
> Of childish innocence while he beside her lay.   (p. 16)

The idyll is soon fractured by 'salt Salacia / Her elder sister' (p. 16). Salacia's jealousy takes a particularly insidious form. Lacking any faith in the beyond, she tempts Perennia in a speech which adroitly inverts the terminology of love and lust:

'Sweet sister,' then she smiled, 'this luxury
Of animals and birds for retinue
May fascinate; but can your Eros be
So radiant that he must hide from you
In stealthy midnight visitings his true
Form? Can he be a pure, immortal child
Such as you say? If he is fine to view,
Why does he hide a body that is mild
And harmless? He may be a beast, gross and defiled,

'For many a satyr has an easy charm
And glowing look, insinuating trust
That merely leads us on to our own harm
Till we are prostituted to its lust
And every passionate and goatish gust
That shudders through its body. Though he fawns
And flatters you with presents, yet you must
Fly from this place before full morning dawns
And listen to the loving voice of one who warns.'   (p. 17)

The ironies are delightful. Salacia can see the birds only in terms of luxury. Her choice of noun tells us much of her. In stanza XXI the 'retinue' had been presented to us in a catalogue of birds directly in the tradition of Guillaume de Lorris and Alanus de Insulis. Chalone's words at the end of *Killing Time* come to mind: 'Birds are divine remembrancers' (p. 70). The single word 'luxury' fills out our understanding of the character of Salacia (Latin *salax* bears the senses both of 'lustful' and of 'that which provokes to lust'). The speech introduces us to a pattern of imagery which might profitably be examined in the plays, and in its spiritual blindness, its absorption in the palpable, it also introduces one of the major themes of the plays.

2

Meeting Ends begins with Agappy's Last Post, and we then witness Ensoff, that 'chancellor of the mind', as he brings the world of the play into being:

A sunshaft strikes the steeple by my room,
Flares the high cock that crowns created day . . .

It sems reasonable to take this as the first of the play's many
allusions to that tradition of Hermeticism which holds such a
fascination for Mr Warner, and for many of the figures in whom
he is most interested—Pico della Mirandola, Ficino, Cornelius
Agrippa, Blake, Samuel Palmer, Yeats. The particular image
we may know from Vaughan's *Cock-Crowing*, for example. In
Hermetic symbolism the cock is an emblem of 'that which tends
towards eternity and which takes care to grant first place to
things of the spirit' (M. M. Davy, *Essai sur la symbolique romane*).
A passage from Ficino's *Commentary on the Symposium* is help-
ful here, too. Ficino compares God and the sun. He explains
that 'Plato says that the light by which the mind might under-
stand everything is that same God by whom everything was
created', and he makes a comparison between God and the sun
insofar as God stands in the same relation to Minds as the sun
does to eyes. 'It is the sun which generates eyes and it is the
sun which gives them the power to see . . . In a similar manner,
God creates the soul and gives to it mind, the power of under-
standing. But for the light of God the mind would be empty and
dark; in that light we can see the principles of everything . . .
So we understand all things through the light of God, but the
pure light itself and its source, we are not able to see in this life.'[1]

The very name of the speaker reassures us that it is not fanci-
ful to read these lines in terms of this hermetic and neo-Platonic
tradition. The name *Ensoff* is a version of the Cabbalistic
'Ensoph'—'the one without end'—the subject of another chapter
('The Concealed God') in Professor Wind's book. Does Ensoff,
then, represent the *deus absconditus*, 'The pure light itself and its
source, we are not able to see in this life', of Renaissance
neo-Platonism? The terms in which Mr Warner's stage direc-
tions introduce him might suggest this. 'Light on ENSOFF, who
is dressed throughout the play in the robe of the Chancellor
of Oxford University. He stands high up on a raised platform,
downstage left, that is quite separate from the main, circular
acting area. Stage itself dark' (p. 1). The emphasis on the
separateness of Ensoff's platform is suggestive, as is his position
looking down upon a circular stage on which poor players are
to strut and fret. But equally suggestive, in a different way, are
his robes. The designated robes suggest, initially, that here is an

[1] My translation.

emblem of learning. However, in the light of what we have seen
already, we probably need to be more specific than this, and
consider Ensoff as a figure representative rather of the Renais-
sance idea of wisdom—a notion intimately bound in with that
of the Contemplative Life. Let us take some evidence from
Mr Warner's text. Callisterne tells us that 'He has a kind of cha-
otic majesty' (p. 4), and the cosmological pun suggests the
Cabbala's creator figure. In I.7 Ensoff is in dialogue with
Agappy:

> AGAPPY: . . . I suppose when you are executed your head
> will dance up and down on the ground like a
> moonbeam.
> ENSOFF: Lose my head?
> AGAPPY: Those robes give you away. You're out of the
> ordinary. *You* can't last long!
> ENSOFF: A Chancellor of the mind?
> AGAPPY: That won't save you.
> ENSOFF: The towns I have called into being and peopled
> with my imagination.

After the revelation of the sundial which closes 2.4, Ensoff is in
dialogue with Wrasse and Callisterne and tells them, 'It's an
unknown God who's come. If you love him, stay with him'
(p. 46). By the end of the play Ensoff has left his raised platform
(to be replaced by Agappy) and utters the unmistakeably human
sentiments:

> The silent stars play havoc with our toys
> But we have kingdoms that they cannot touch.   (p. 47)

Ensoff is, then, at one point in the play a 'chancellor of the
mind' who talks of the creative force of his imagination. Taken
against the background of Renaissance neo-Platonism all this
suggests that Ensoff is best seen as Renaissance magus. He
belongs, that is to say, in the tradition of *magia* developed out of
the alleged writings of Hermes Trismegistus by such figures as
Pico and Ficino and given its most complete expression by
Cornelius Agrippa in his *De occulta philosophia*—a work which
Mr Warner has edited. We may take the hint to see Ensoff as
magus from some other lines in the prologue which glance at
the magi:

But higher than the not yet risen lark
Three wise men from the west reach for the moon . . .

As magus he will necessarily be a man apart. 'The wise man, who has knowledge of the secrets of nature, is secret and spiritual. He lives alone, far from the common mob. Placed high above other men, he is unique, free, absolute, tranquil, pacific, immobile, simple, collected, one. He needs no one' (Carolus Bovillus, *De Sapiente*).[2] That, at any rate, is the idea. Ensoff assumes initially that the contemplative life is a sufficient end in itself, that it is enough for his lamp to be seen at midnight hour in some high lonely tower. The working out of the play suggests, however, that this is an end that will not meet his needs.

Ensoff, as mage, is both God-figure (the mage as theurgist controls both self and nature) and, by an analogy common and natural to neo-Platonism, the poet. It is a central tenet of Renaissance neo-Platonism that human creative powers are analogous to divine powers. Ficino's *Theologia platonica* argues that where God creates in the world by means of His thought, the poet conceives within himself the intellectual species (forms which are the definition of a plurality of objects of the same class) and expresses them by making a copy in earthly materials —the work of art. *Meeting Ends* may be about Ensoff's 'chaotic majesty', but it is also about the imagination's attempt to turn chaos into coherent symbolic language.

3

The first of Ensoff's creations is that revealed to us by the dawning light which begins scene one: '. . . three women, each with her head and hands in a pillory. AGAPPY downstage right . . . WRASSE upstage . . . CALLISTERNE . . . downstage left.' To these women there enters Shango, nude save for his bull's head. He kisses Callisterne chastely, tears Wrasse's swimming costume from her, and bows before Agappy, doffing the bull's head. What we witness is an act of choice made by this mysterious nude man. As yet we know nothing of him, though the bull's head may offer some suggestions. Purely as a stage

2 My translation.

spectacle the scene is resonant but enigmatic. It is only in the light of evidence from elsewhere in the play that we can attempt some kind of elucidation. The characters' names offer a convenient point of entrance.

Agappy is clearly a version of Agape. In pre-biblical Greek *eros* denotes ecstatic passion while the verb *agapan* and noun *agapesis* denote a cooler emotion, a love based on rational preference. The form *agape* is, I believe, unknown before the Septuagint. As used there it denotes a love whose definition would have to find room for the doctrine of fidelity. *Agape* as used in the Gospels and above all in the Pauline and Johannine epistles refers to beneficent love, love which is unselfish and seeks only the good of others. It is theocentric, since it is the reproduction of God's own 'outgoing' love. It is frequently translated by the Church Fathers as *caritas*. *Eros*, on the other hand, is egocentric, love directed to the pursuit of some object to be acquired for the self, love which seeks to possess or control. If we are right to see Agappy as Mr Warner's version of *agape*, then we should expect these distinctions to operate in discriminating between this character and the other two women who share the stage with her. This the text confirms. Agappy tells Wrasse, '(*Gently*) If you accept something as good, then you choose it' (p. 13), and at the close of the three-part polyphony which constitutes I.2 she has the final words: 'We are the unknown ones whom all men know. When we please we are fulfilled. In our birth, sorrow is our deepest joy. We are beaten but not killed. Poor, we bring wealth to others; inheritors of nothing but the world' (p. 13). We know that Agappy is unmarried and childless and we may remember that in the early days of the Church the Agapetae were Virgins dedicated to God. Ensoff tells her that she lacks 'the grimmer virtues' (p. 27) and her injunction is to 'Prove your power by throwing it away' (p. 28), an injunction which comes after a long scene in which we have seen Wrasse endeavour to prove *her* sexual power by exercising it over Shango. Agappy's long soliloquy which constitutes I.10 offers further confirmation: 'I made a man's love the centre of my life . . . When it failed, chaos came. Ah well! Love comes and goes, but friendship stays . . . He said 'Nice to take you to the theatre this evening.' . . . 'Be charitable,' he said. Well, I thought, chastity stirs the passion it's supposed to restrain! But an act of faith is an act of love' (pp. 32–33). It is not, then, surprising to find Agappy telling us and Ensoff 'I was never a good hater' (p. 44) and, as an inevitable corollary of that remark, she tells Ensoff 'I long ago became aware that a life lived solely for human rewards was shallow' (p. 45).

The figure who stands in most direct opposition, morally and thematically, is Wrasse. Again the name helps us. The Wrasse is a cleaner-fish, that is, it eats parasites from the skin and inside the gills and mouths of other fish. Wrasses are territorial creatures, living in well-defined groups of eight to ten individuals. Within each group there is only one male, the rest of the group consisting of a harem of mature females, and a number of immature females. The male is the dominant force of the group, and there is a hierarchy of dominance among the females. What is remarkable, though, is what happens in the eventuality of the dominant male's death. Within an hour or two the leader of the female hierarchy begins to take over the male role, and simultaneously she begins to change sex. In behavioural terms she does this quite quickly. A physiological change follows. The female wrasse is, in fact, a kind of hermaphrodite. In their female state they have small quantities of testicular material in their ovaries. Once the behavioural change triggers off the physiological change the gonad is taken over by the testicular material, and the egg-producing elements degenerate. Within a matter of weeks the new male is producing sperm. One particularly interesting feature of wrasse society follows from this. The male usually directs the greater part of his aggression towards the female(s) he imagines to be most likely to change sex in this way. It is scarcely surprising that Mr Warner should find in this fish an apposite point of reference for that theme of the conflict of sexual roles which runs all the way through the *Requiem* trilogy. The theme is perhaps seen at its clearest in *Lying Figures*, where Gonad actually appears as a character. (It is perhaps worth noting that Wrasse completes the sequence of fish names begun by Guppy and Squaloid). Within *Meeting Ends* it is in the relationship of Wrasse and Shango that we see this particular theme treated most fully. Wrasse's opening word of the play is a simple 'Men' (p. 3) and her preoccupation with the power game of gender is rapidly made clear ('Let alone, men are literally inconceivable' (p. 3)). It is she who talks of 'the post-marital

bloodbath' (p. 4) and who sees marriage in terms of dominance
and submission: 'Maternity. Forced labour and endless penal
servitude' (p. 5). Still, she is far from submitting to the 'penal
servitude' (the pun is a favourite Joycean one)—she has other
ideas: 'Any woman can get control over a man, simply by
flattering his ego and placing a hand on his genitals' (p. 5).
Dominance, it seems, comes naturally to her: 'I was a bully at
school' (p. 7). As the dominant female in a school of cleaner-fish
Wrasse's remark carries the ring of truth. As that dominant
female she can be expected, as we have seen, to take the final
step towards the top of the hierarchy. The idea is already present
in her mind: 'I love the idea of a ruthless brute of a husband
eating and drinking all those things that will ultimately put his
wife in his place' (p. 7). Even so she is aware that the battle can
only be won at the cost of losing those pleasures which are pro-
duced by the tensions of the conflict itself: 'I don't want to lose
my new man, neither do I want to whine after him. Anyway,
if I could control him I'd lose interest . . . I've got to have him'
(pp. 10–11). When we first see this particular battle of wills and
wits, in I.3, it is Shango who appears to have the upper hand.
His fatuous flattery delights the shallow Wrasse. He sees the
long-range courtship of Wrasse and the completion of the *Times*
crossword as analogous problems. He succeeds in both: 'A kiss
(*Fills in a clue on crossword. To audience*). Won across' (p. 18). But
we are aware that for all his apparent dominance he speaks from
a seat within a mousetrap. When the next scene opens the trap
has been sprung, the mouse caught and given his mouse's wheel
on which to play. Wrasse has achieved the transfer of power—
and has in the terms of the cleaner fish completed her sex-
change—she enters dressed as a ring*master*, in top hat, morning-
dress coat and tights. She carries the appropriate whip. Mr
Warner's imagination has lighted on one of those transvestite
figures who populate so densely the stages of popular entertain-
ment. Wrasse is committed wholeheartedly to sensuality. She
believes it to be her source of power: 'I can always twist the boss
round my finger by letting him have a little feel' (p. 19). How-
ever, the first two scenes of the second Act suggest how in-
adequate this is as a base for power. She is characterized (and
dressed) throughout as a woman of gaudy banality. Her dia-
logues with Shango (notably in I.4.) and her soliloquy in II.1

are couched in an idiolect of relentless triteness. She is well summed up by her dress of shocking pink and her addiction to bubble-gum. In the polyphony of I.1. she remarks, 'The trouble with the senses is not that they give pleasure but that it doesn't last' (p. 4). The remark takes us back, curiously enough, to neo-Platonism. It takes us back, indeed, to Ficino, via, perhaps, Professor Wind. Professor Wind's fourth chapter reminds us that 'As Ficino was never tired of repeating, the trouble about the pleasures of the senses is not that they are pleasures but that they do not last'. Clearly Ficino is not alone in finding the aphorism worthy of repetition. Ficino's most extended consideration of the aphorism's implications is to be found in his *De voluptate* and *Apologus de voluptate*. This latter contains a fable narrating how True Pleasure, which originally dwelt on earth, has been translated to Heaven, and her place on earth taken by a deceptive imitation, False Pleasure. But properly understood False Pleasure can be seen as a reflection of True Pleasure. The distinction corresponds roughly to that between Aphrodite Urania and Aphrodite Pandemos. Wrasse is Mr Warner's false, or earthly, *voluptas*.

We have, in Agappy (Love) and Wrasse (Pleasure), two members of the Three Graces, so important a motif in Florentine neo-Platonism. The third member we should expect to be *pulchritudo*. The pattern is thus completed logically when the third figure in Ensoff's tableau is discovered to be Callisterne— or, in Greek, 'the beautiful-breasted one'. We can now see that the three women with whom the action of the play begins are the Warnerian version of the Three Graces.

4

To understand the thematic implications of Ensoff's tableau we need to examine the relationship between Ensoff ('the Beyond') and each of these three women.

Agappy's relationship with Ensoff appears to be the most complete—at any rate when the play begins. It is to her that the others turn for information about him:

CALLISTERNE: (*Brightly*)   I always think when I see Ensoff 'He's so sweet he must do unspeakable things in bed.'

WRASSE: (*To Agappy*)   Does he? (p. 4)

Agappy knows, like any good neo-Platonist or follower of the pseudo-Dionysus (or, indeed, like any reader of Ensoff's own book—the Cabbala), that the lesson is 'To be initiated, close your eyes' (p. 7). Or as Agrippa puts it, under the marginal note, *Cur Amor caecus*: 'Ideoque amorem Orpheus sine oculis describit, quia est supra intellectum.' Only she is fit to blow Reveille.

Wrasse has, as we have seen, made a very different choice. Ficinian argument insists that since sensual pleasures are transitory (but decidedly pleasurable) they should be viewed as images of less mutable delights. The sexual language used between Ensoff and Agappy recognizes this—as indeed does one of the central traditions of Christian mysticism. For Wrasse, however, sexual ecstasy is never an image of transcendence. Rather it is a means to mundane power of a very delusive kind, or, in an allusion to *The Shipman's Tale*, it becomes a 'currency': 'I had an overdraft of sixty-eight pounds on the housekeeping . . . He said he'd pay it if I wrote out in my own hand a list of things I would do to him and let him do to me, and their various prices, so I could write off the debt. He pinned it above the bed and made me pay every penny' (pp. 38–39). In one case we are in the world of the *fabliau*, in the other we are in the world of Richard of St Victor's Spiritual Marriage. The events of the play offer Wrasse the possibility of change. In II.3 she is beginning to learn the limitations of sexual power. Unlike her fishy namesake the change of sex and sex-role cannot be complete ('*Damn* the menstrual clock' (p. 42)). Her frustration and depression are vented in jealous suspicions (true to the fabliau world) of Callisterne:

CALLISTERNE: You are distraught.
WRASSE: Have you no feelings?
CALLISTERNE: For what?
WRASSE: For me. You've enough for my man

(p. 43).

Callisterne suggests, 'Let's go and be with Ensoff. He's wise, and understanding.' She is invited, in the words of the epigraph to *Perennia*, to look 'towards the Beyond as the true goal of ecstasy'. In II.5 we find that Wrasse and Callisterne have made the journey. Wrasse's sensual banality is at least partly hidden. She

enters 'with a cloak of muted colour over her bright dress'
(p. 45). They enter immediately after Ensoff has, in his gesture
of revelation, uncovered the sundial. Wrasse has reached the
moment of choice, but is unable or unwilling to choose:

WRASSE: What shall I do, Ensoff?
ENSOFF: It's an unknown God who's come. If you love
him, stay with him. (*Pause*) If you both wish.
WRASSE: I wish for both. (p. 46)

Callisterne has made her own choice much earlier. As early as
I.2 she asserts, 'It was Ensoff who changed my mind' (p. 4). In
her weakness, isolation, and beauty, as we see it in I.8, she, just
as importantly, does something to change Ensoff's mind, as his
beautiful lyric in I.9 makes clear. Wrasse may be unable to
make her choice here in II.5, but Callisterne's position is clear
enough, as is her acceptance by Ensoff:

CALLISTERNE: And me? I hardly dare speak to you, as I
think of you as a father.
ENSOFF: I will not importune, nor yet desert you.
I am your close friend and will never hurt
you. (p. 46)

It is at this point that Shango enters, razor in hand. Just as
Wrasse's spiritual blindness found expression in jealousy, so does
Shango's—'Hands off my woman' (p. 46). He, at least, is in
doubt as to which choice Wrasse might make. The castration
completed, Callisterne and Ensoff act out a conclusion of great
dignity and serenity, with debts both to Lear and Cordelia and
Oedipus and Antigone. The conclusion's heightened lyrical
language can only fitly be followed by the symbolic musical
language of the Reveille.

5

Of the dramatis personae only Shango remains undiscussed.
How does he fit into these symbolic and thematic patterns? His
name is that of a Yoruba God. He is the God of thunder and
lightning, of hunting and pillage. He is said to have had the
power of invoking fire from the heavens, but with Promethean

results. The fire destroyed every other member of his family and in agonies of self-reproach he hanged himself. Other Promethean allusions are common in the *Requiem* plays, and we need not look far for the reason. Renaissance humanism makes much use of Prometheus as a symbol of all-embracing wisdom, and of the adventurous effort to possess it. For many Humanists Prometheus is an entirely admirable figure. Budé, for example, writes: 'I believe that Prometheus is the philosophic intellect which, once it has mastered natural science, astronomy, and the other branches of philosophy, is able to rise with assurance to a knowledge of divine things' (*De Studio literarum recte et commode instituendo*).[3] But for Agrippa in the *De Vanitate* Prometheus seems better understood as a symbol of human presumption, of the failure of Humanism. It is in such a context that Agrippa makes use of a pseudo-Pauline saying of much relevance to Mr Warner's plays—'The Ignorante arise, and take the Kingedome of Heaven: and we with our learninge, fall headlonge into Hell.'[4]

Shango, in his soliloquy spoken during his Promethean tortures (I.6), learns enough to end, 'Help us grapple with the frailties of our apprehension' (p. 26). Before this he has echoed the more usual Renaissance interpretation of his rôle: 'I am a man wracked by doubts but capable of glimpses of perfection' (p. 13). One is reminded of a classic formulation of the divided nature of Renaissance Humanism, to be found in Sidney's *Apology*: 'our erected wit maketh us to know what perfection is, and yet our infected will keepeth us from reaching unto it.' (The *Apology* is echoed more directly elsewhere in *Meeting Ends* when Agappy reminisces: 'When I was young I was so beautiful I kept old men from play and young women from the chimney-corner' (p. 32)). It is around the polarities of this formulation that Mr Warner's plays are structured.

6

Shango's castration of Ensoff marks the jealous failure of Promethean aspirations, of Humanist presumption. Its Christian overtones are evident, as an act of spiritual blindness, but we must not overlook its implicit allusion to the castration of

---

[3] My translation.
[4] I quote from the 1569 English translation.

Uranus. In Hesiod's *Theogony* the legend is related that the heavenly Aphrodite (Aphrodite Urania) arose from the foam of the sea produced by the castration of Uranus. Once more Professor Wind's masterly exegesis of neo-Platonic thinking is of great help here:

> The castration of Uranus is of one type with the dismember-ment of Osiris, Attis, Dionysus, all of which signify the same mystery to the neo-Orphic theologians: for whenever the supreme One descends to the Many, this act of creation is imagined as a sacrificial agony, as if the One were cut to pieces and scattered. Creation is conceived in this way as a cosmogonic death, by which the concentrated power of one deity is offered up and dispersed: but the descent and diffusion of the divine power are followed by its resurrection, when the Many are 'recollected' into the One.[5]

Most neo-Platonic allegorizers concentrate exclusively on the castration's production of Aphrodite Urania. Most forget (con-veniently) that the castration also produced the Furies and a brood of monstrous giants. The events of Mr Warner's plays suggest that he does not forget this.

7

Sidney's neo-Platonic formulation has a pleasing balance about it:

> our erected wit maketh us know what perfection is, and yet our infected will keepeth us from reaching unto it.

In the *Requiem* trilogy the balance is less perfect. Sexual erec-tions are more prominent than erections of wit. The degree to which the will is infected can hardly be exaggerated. The imagery of venereal disease permeates *Lying Figures*. Or consider the dramatis personae of *Killing Time*. One character (Kuru) bears the name of a degenerative disease of the brain, endemic amongst certain cannibal tribes, and apparently spread by the ritual cannibalization of brain tissue. Another (Phagocyte) is named after a leucocyte which, under certain limited conditions, has the power to defend the system against infection by absorb-ing pathogenic microbes. A third (Chalone) carries the name of

[5] Edgar Wind, *ibid.*, p. 133.

an internal secretion which inhibits the action of certain organs
and tissues. With characteristic ambiguity Chalone's name
is also suspiciously close to the Greek τὸ καλόν—the morally
beautiful, the *summum bonum*. The ambiguity is significant.
For Renaissance neo-Platonism the psychomachia (*Killing Time*
takes place within the human brain) was a battle to be fought
out in the best Prudentian tradition. Man had the freedom and
the capacity to make a rational choice. In *Requiem* the psycho-
machia belongs as much to human biochemistry as to Pruden-
tius. Moral theology's territory has been partly usurped by
neurotheology, to borrow a word of Aldous Huxley's.

Cornelius Agrippa moved from a belief that knowledge was
power to a belief rather that 'There is nothing in this world,
which is not corrupted, nor any learning which is not abused . . .
Nothing can chaunce unto man more pestilente, then know-
ledge: this is the very pestilence, that putteth all mankinde to
ruine'. More than the will is infected. The *Requiem* trilogy seems
more than once to demand a comparison with Shakespeare's
last plays. If those plays seem at times to embody the world of
the *De Occulta*, *Meeting Ends* inhabits rather the world of the
De Vanitate. The Three Graces have been put in the pillory,
Vitruvian man doubles as a pet mouse. In *Meeting Ends* the
Brothel at Mytilene looms larger than the isle of sounds and
sweet airs; the snowdrops are still no more than a hope as the
Requiem ends.

6

Paul Hewison

Theology in the Plays

'Now don't go and bring in religion.' (*Maquettes*, p. 32)

In the beginning of Act III of *Lying Figures*, Gonad is seated 'in the vulva of a hollow tree-trunk . . . pierced by sharpened metal stakes . . . Within the trunk, four stones hang from just above his head on a wheel . . . so that each time he moves he runs the risk either of being impaled or of being severely bruised.' The image is that of St Maron, one of the Desert Fathers: it is derived from an eighteenth-century engraving of this determinedly holy person, reproduced in one of Mr Warner's favourite books, *The God-Possessed*, by Jacques Lacarrière. The source is significant: for Lacarrière is not a theologian at all, but approaches the mystic, ascetic world of the third-century Thebaid in a spirit of aesthetic fascination and ironic detachment: his master in this land is Anatole France. This at once raises the problem of Mr Warner's attitude to his own theological material: his plays abound in biblical quotations; but are they any more than quotations? After all, they are from the Authorized Version, which no self-respecting theologian even looks at nowadays. Perhaps their interest is merely literary or aesthetic; or at most they serve as ironical contrasts to the even more frequent sexual puns, innuendos and images. Is one really justified in going and bringing in religion?

The very title of the central trilogy, *Requiem*, might suggest a positive answer: but it is also wise to glance at *Maquettes*, since models for projects reveal the nature of the problems to be tackled, perhaps solved, and therefore obscured, in the major work: the maker's thumb-marks can be seen in the clay but not in the marble. The first play, *Emblems*, sets the somewhat sordid realities of sexual desire beside the empty ceremonies of marriage: only when the brides are stripped is any truth revealed, and this appears to be Lesbianism anyway. Similarly, the biblical references are either meaningless or flippant:

BRIDE ONE: Holy Mother of God!
BRIDE TWO: The Mother of God must also have been His
               daughter.

The conclusion, however, introduces a new element: man is not
simply sexual and godless, but doomed to die, and aware of it:

> Beneath this scalp within this skin a skull
> Out of which peer two globes that clutch the light.

The skeleton, the dust, the dirt, recall a Jacobean *memento mori*:
but the real reference is to Eliot. Mr Warner sees the skull
beneath the skin. Show him a handful of dust and he'll show
you fear. Yet this land is not entirely waste, although only the
last line of the play hints it:

> Dusk brings the darkness, embers mark the end,
> Yet what contortion leaps the . . . thrush's . . . throat?

Troat immediately crushes that hope. The Old Man reacts to
the corrupt frivolity of human nature by destroying it. This is
not because he cannot understand the sexual urge; indeed he
justifies it, and how better than by quoting Restoration comedy:

> Because a man lies with a woman once, must he the rest of his
> life?

The trouble is that he has standards, even though they are ruth-
less, military ones, and even though they make him a solitary
figure:

> I have been part of a regiment, and am now alone.

Moreover, these standards have a theological dimension. The
other characters' off-hand religious remarks are no longer
allowed to remain as such: 'Good God!' exclaims the Woman:
'You have great faith', replies the Old Man. Again:

YOUNG MAN: Oh my God.
OLD MAN: Why hast thou forsaken the lot of us? Kill
               on, boy, kill on. Christ was a fisher.
WOMAN: Now don't go and bring in religion.
YOUNG MAN: Christ was a fisher?
OLD MAN: A dexterous and a sinister one.

The references to the Crucifixion, Death and the Last Judgement are enough to indicate how the play will end. A moment later, 'The boss' is actually under discussion: the Old Man regards him as 'a bloody fool'; the Woman had heard he's 'in a very bad way'; and the Boy treats us to another of Christ's psalm quotations during the Passion, and a definitive statement: 'Oh, he's finished. He's dead.' The Woman makes an exceptionally fatuous sentimental remark, and then a cock crows. Nobody, unfortunately, goes out and weeps bitterly. Instead, the ensuing mockery of the Prayer-Book, naturally enough of its marriage regulations, reaches its inevitable conclusion as the Boy states in biblical language and 'as though reading lesson' the state of mind of the Old Man:

> And the Lord saw man as beautiful and imperfect, and stripping away the imperfections found only a shadow of the man he had thought so beautiful.

To men who are imperfect, who have betrayed and denied God, and then invoke Light in the *Nunc Dimittis*, the Light can come in only one form. Red-hot coals are heaped upon their heads. The Crucified Redeemer is indeed dead; the Old Testament God of Wrath is not.

The very title of *Lumen* indicates that the problem is to be further explored: *is* there a Light shining in the darkness, and if so, what kind of Light? At first, the vision of the earlier plays seems confirmed: man, dominated by sex, must view himself as a hunk of bacon, and therefore even if God did become Incarnate, it was only into this corruption:

ACTOR: Dung.
ACTRESS: That word!
ACTOR: Made flesh; stable produce.
ACTRESS: Bacon.

The same manipulation of St John's 'And the Word was made Flesh' recurs in Actor's summary of human life and procreation:

> Flesh, words, promise kept under pressure, result—new flesh, words, flesh, word, flesh grows up and then all the fumbling and bumbling all over a-fondling-gain.

It is no surprise to be told that 'The marriage licence is a charter for violation', and finally that 'we fall, all of us, in exactly the same way'. However, it is precisely after this confession that Actress can state: 'That for which we grieve should make us rejoice', meaning the *felix culpa*, the Fall which produced the Passion; and that 'our knowledge is curtailed lest we should despair', indicating at least an interested Controller of Mankind, and hinting at the problem of Prescience which will re-emerge in later plays. Thus even though the ensuing action reinforces the identification of Man and Baconmeat, of Sex and Violence, Actor can still light a candle, an old flame which is not just a mistress but 'That which distinguishes us from the brute creation, Old as the crags, The vultures, the pain'. The Promethean references may indicate that only through suffering, indeed through challenging a God of Wrath, can mankind gain anything to set him above the beasts: at all events, this Lumen is a Spark, not the Word: this is Gnosticism, not Christianity.

Actor and Actress try, and fail, to touch hands:

ACTOR: We have left it too late.
ACTRESS: We shouldn't have joked.
ACTOR: Darken our lightness.
ACTRESS: Bear with our weakness.

On stage, the actors become baconmeat and then become nothing. The feeling here is close to that at the climax of *Love's Labour's Lost*. Jokes and lightness, in morals and in mind, are not enough in the face of darkness and death. Endless puns on Bacon leave a nasty taste in the mouth after the Promethean vision reveals what the Bacon means. The words of Mercury are harsh after the songs of Apollo.

The problem remains, which way to go. The *Requiem* trilogy takes up all the themes proposed in *Maquettes*: marriage, sex, violence and human folly, contrasted at once with an Angry God and a Crucified Christ. The first play, *Lying Figures*, leaves no doubt as to which theme will dominate it: the epigraph is Genesis VII: 4: 'And I will wipe off the face of the earth every living thing that I have made.' The first two Acts re-state the reasons for the wrath of the Almighty: in Epigyne we have another faithless bride, for 'What is a wedding but a white lie?' and even corpses retain that dual obsession with sex and puns: a clinch is the fatal Cleopatra for which they lose the world, and

are content to lose it. Mr Warner's Lazarus can rise only in a
sexual sense. Their puns indeed link sex, death and religion, as
in Laz's 'Jesus! body-snatchers. There's a stone missing', until
Sapphira's invocation of Mr Warner's own trilogy, 'Let us sing
a requiem for the living!' recognizes that Life is Death, if Life
is only Sex. She does not realize that her conclusion, 'The way
to stop transmission of death is to call a halt to procreation', is
precisely the justification for the Genesis quotation. The entrance
of Death with his scythe at the end of Act II seems, if anything,
delayed.

Yet other notes have been struck: Gonad in Act I finds some
consolation in the beauty of nature and even decides: 'there's a
lot to be said for watching the dead'; Epigyne has a suitably
Augustinian attitude to promiscuity: 'God forbid we should
ever lose our sense of guilt.' Act III, as we have seen, begins
promisingly: Gonad is emulating the blessed Maron, and pray-
ing he won't die an atheist. The twists and turns of the scene,
however, soon prevent any simple identification of Gonad as
Soul and Epigyne as Body. Firstly, as the latter informs the
former, 'in spite of your religiosity, you have a mistress'. It
might seem that the ensuing recognition of each other's fault
will, as in *Lumen*, bring about reconciliation: they do admit that
'Marriage makes strange bed-fellows': but Gonad is next in-
formed that his wife's lover is his boss, and that is how he
obtained his job. His comment is as much on his religious as his
personal life: 'Not to know, yourself, yet to be known. That's the
real torture.' The boss, Guppy, adopts a realistic cynicism
which appears the only logical reaction to life as we are discover-
ing it to be: 'It's the innocent that suffer. The only way to avoid
suffering is to be guilty . . . Our bodies are nothing, therefore we
may as well abuse them . . . Without Judas you cannot have
heroism . . . When God hammered out the world he arrived at
chaos.' Yet this almost Satanic, or at least Manichaean, position
is refuted at the next twist of the plot: with the discovery that
his own wife is in turn Gonad's mistress, the cynical Guppy exits
screaming, the astonished and astonishing words 'Benevolent
Christ!' on his lips. Epigyne gives us the moral:

Each man has two women, each woman two men. All eight
of us poisoned by delight.

We return to the Fall: Lilith and Eve, Satan and Adam, the attractive and rotten apple encountered in Act II. The last scene, as the religious and treacherous Gonad 'proves his manhood' by using the razor on the naked Xyster, finally unites the images of cruelty, sex, love and death into a climax where any optimism or lyricism is inappropriate.

Act IV remorselessly gives us the theological consequences. The corpses continue as before, and their assumptions over Sex, Life and Death have been confirmed by the rest of the play. Once more the God of Wrath is justified, and even commended:

LAZ: God is ruthless.
SAPPH: Ruthless? Don't you mean pitiful?
LAZ: Exactly.

The kindest thing to do to humanity is to exterminate it. The following lines all identify childbirth with death, the Crucifixion with the Nativity with the culminating image of the Slaughter of the Innocents: we are reminded of the neo-Platonic conclusion, that it is better not to be born. Such a fate, indeed, has apparently been that of Gonad's own child. The candle imagery from *Lumen* recurs but rather differently. Gonad extinguishes one candle, and attempts to mourn the baby with the other: but 'Emptiness enfolds. Darkness encroaches on the light, and in lightness we dare not comprehend.' *Maquettes* ended in prayer, even if it was an ironic inversion of the Evensong invocation; *Lying Figures* ends with despair, the total inversion of St John's optimism, deepened by the shift to the modern meaning of 'comprehend'. In the darkness of our folly, we cannot understand God, Who therefore in His Justice and Pity sends us out into the darkness of death. Gonad exits with the candle, 'taking with him the only source of light'.

This conclusion to *Lying Figures* nevertheless begs many theological questions. The darkness appears to be at once the cause, the symptom and the effect of Man's estrangement from God. It is thus inescapable, and even predestined. Surely God then must take some kind of responsibility? The next two plays therefore investigate the relationship between God and His Creation: they both contain God-like figures, Chalone and Ensoff, who at first stand outside and comment on the action, but gradually become involved with it. Their Incarnations, however, are very different.

Killing Time is only ostensibly about war, the ultimate symbol of the judgement which God in effect lets man pass on himself. Squaloid explains:

> It's not war you should fear. It's fear. Every man's a brute underneath,

and Kuru develops this:

> They make a society based on fear; fear of breakdown of law and of outside enemies. Create an army . . . that cultivates death as a means of enforcement. This leads to war, and so to the collapse of the very society that had created it for its own protection!

We are reminded of Rochester's verdict on Man:

> For fear he armes, and is of Armes afraid,
> By fear, to fear, successively betray'd . . .
> The good he acts, the ill he does endure,
> 'Tis all for fear, to make himself secure.
> Meerly for safety, after Fame we thirst,
> For all Men, wou'd be *Cowards* if they durst.

Similarly Chalone's 'lecture' on the human brain emphasizes that its 'only moral direction . . . is towards survival', and that it is man's capacity to commit suicide which distinguishes him from the animals. He grants that: 'you can argue that this ability of man also implies its opposite, and that—may—save us from the holocaust'; but he has earlier remarked: 'Perhaps there is a greatness in man only brought out in war. What a frail hope.' It is this hope which the play first raises, and then dashes.

For there does seem to be hope by the end of Act I. Men are still seen as fallen, are indeed hailed as Luciferian figures, light-bearers in the worst sense:

QUARK: (*to the men*) How art thou fallen from Heaven!
KURU: Morning, son.

Significantly, on the same page, we are kept on our theological toes by puns on the three major religious writers of the century, Karl Barth, Paul Tillich and Bonhoeffer. The fate of the latter seems to reinforce the emerging theme: that wisdom, truth and beauty are best created precisely from suffering. This is the 'opposite' which Chalone saw implied in man's capacity for suicide. Therefore, indeed, we should not give up hope. Squaloid tells us: 'It's the only preservative.' Quark is to be guillotined because she has been 'found guilty of despair'. Yet she does not die: the guillotine is harmless. Quark's reaction is rapturous optimism:

> The universe spins on a shaft of light
>   Whose name is love,

and Kuru states the essential theme:

> Strength is a beauty only known in grief:
>   Like men at war
> Who find true comradeship in cruelty,
>   And bravery
> Even as they mourn the very friends they kill—
> So may this night of parting bind us still.

Unfortunately, this solution takes no account of a God who is likely to have moral standards. The Old Man in *Troat* had standards; and he was a soldier. Act II, Scene V brings us back to heaven: the de Lassus Requiem begins and Chalone enters with a devastating series of quotations from the Old Testament God of Wrath. 'Fear, and the pit, and the snare shall be upon thee.' Chalone does pray for Mercy; but admits that 'the hour of our going . . . is of no moment in the dazzling eyes of God'. The action quickly confirms the threat. Kuru commits suicide: it was inevitable that somebody would. Quark is blinded, and responds with 'God is best seen when all the sky is dark', a one-line summary of *Samson Agonistes* which might be a restatement of her theme of wisdom through suffering; or might equally well be a comment on the nature of God. Phagocyte is shot, ironically not just for being a spy and taking Squaloid's girl, but also because Squaloid is keeping his word to him. Worst of all, the God-figure Chalone undergoes a Crucifixion which turns out to be a joke and a cheat. The theological overtones are certainly there: before his 'Passion', Chalone defines the Trinity: 'That which is one is one . . . That which is not one is also one'; during it, he prays in words from the Psalms: 'Keep me as the apple of an eye, under the shadow of thy wing'; Squaloid actually advises him: 'Just think of yourself as the suffering servant.' Yet Chalone is merely acting. This God does not suffer for humanity: he deceives it, so that it can condemn itself. Nevertheless, Chalone is embarrassed by his own Pitilessness. He tries to claim that: 'Sympathy is innocence', only to be answered by Squaloid: 'Sympathy is impotence.' He appeals to Quark, who has suffered a genuine Passion, to do his own work for him: 'Let your love lighten upon the waste of our wraths and sorrows.' Finally, he expounds his position: 'one prays, of course. But the thought always returns; he saved others, himself he cannot save.' By accepting the crowd's view of Christ on the Cross, Chalone denies, not only the Resurrection, but the Passion itself. The only reason for believing Christ could not, and did not, save himself, is to believe that He was not God, either because He never was (as in Mohammedanism), or because His Divine Nature left him before the Crucifixion (as in, by different methods, Nestorianism and Monophysitism). Quite simply, God is not on the Cross, because God doesn't belong on crosses. Chalone does not really suffer, because his job is to judge the world. 'Withdrawal of sympathy is essential if one is to get anything done.' God cannot come out of His heaven precisely because all is not right with the world.

The play can only end in a prayer. The light imagery is there, as ever: but it is given its 'musical equivalent'—a cockcrow, of course; and there are no candles, only 'the flames of matches'—which blow out. There has been some consolation in the play: the beauty and wisdom which comes from suffering. Yet the eternal problem of all tragedy from *Oedipus* to *Lear* remains: what is the use of beauty and wisdom if you are blind or dead? Any answer must come from God: and God in *Killing Time* is imprisoned in His own nature. The epigraph provides the clue: I Corinthians XV: 56: 'The strength of sin is the law.' A God who involves Himself with His Creation must be a God of Wrath: if He ceased to punish sin, He would cease to be God. An Incarnate God like Chalone actually *increases* Man's suffering, since he must impose the law for sin, measure for measure, and is unwilling to achieve Atonement by suffering himself. The solution is there in Shakespeare's play: but in *Measure for*

Measure the Duke is a Christ-figure; in *Killing Time*, Chalone is an Allah-figure.

The situation in *Meeting Ends* is more promising. The epigraph is Job XIX: 26: 'Yet in my flesh shall I see God', hinting at a true Incarnation and indeed a bodily Resurrection. The character Agappy, clearly St Paul's ἀγάπη, Charity, continually affirms utterly Christian concepts. She outflanks the problems of Predestination by insisting that Man is a free agent: 'Man is a responsible agent, freely choosing disaster'; and again: 'If you accept something as good, then you choose it.' The imagery of the candles, not even lit in the last play, blazes with a significant new light in her words: 'Immortality! It's a box where the flames of blown-out candles are stored.' Modern theologians are suitably mocked: 'He found there was no God, and couldn't understand why he wasn't given a Nobel prize for theology.' All this is confirmed by Shango's attitude to Agappy: he kneels before her 'in homage'. Shango is indeed, like Gonad, the archetypal Warnerian Everyman: 'I am a man wracked by doubts but capable of glimpses of perfection.' Even his cleverest comments are delivered from inside a Mousetrap; his position inside the double wheel is a sordid parody of the neo-Platonic Renaissance artist's view of Man, the perfect symmetrical creature; he can express the utmost cynicism: 'Virtue is largely self-interest'; yet the whole of his soliloquy in Act I Scene VI is a terrified appeal to the Almighty: 'Oh God why don't you exist? . . . I'm looking in the mirror . . . Man is but a thing of nought. Jesus! . . . There is a God after all! . . . If there is a God he lies in the teeth of pain.' The ambiguity of the final pun expresses Shango's perception perfectly: he does indeed see through a glass darkly.

Ensoff, like Shango, is impressed by Agappy: his conversations with her, although sexual on the obvious level, are in effect a discussion of the proper relationship God should have with His Creation. At first he affirms the distance between the two: like Chalone, he has the remoteness of Allah; and like Chalone, he has just returned from war. He does 'love all creative energy', but tells Agappy she lacks 'the grimmer virtues'; he considers that 'God's love for man is the supreme expression of injustice'. All this is changed by his vision of Callisterne in Act I Scene VIII: in effect he falls in love with

her, in what may be described as a neo-Platonic sense. This is
despite, or perhaps because of, her behaviour, which shows man-
kind at its most basic. Her prayer, for which she does not cross
herself—not surprisingly since Ensoff's Crucifixion has yet to
take place—is merely the statement of dry scientific fact. Yet
the conclusion is hardly pure science: 'We rely on multiple
integration.' No man is an island, nor can God be, if He is to
become Man. Like Prospero, whom he closely resembles, Ensoff
must leave the island of his self-centred power, especially in so
far as it is oriented towards vengeance. He can no longer refuse
to acknowledge that Agappy, and Ariel, make ethical demands
or that Callisterne, and Miranda, are to be wondered at:

> Yet should I think
> That there was no mistake—this was for me?
> Within whose skull old wary spiders prey
> And for whose throat a grey bird whets its beak?
> Sure, it can't be
> Unless the world's grown young and lost dismay
> And tears can laugh, and softest touch will stay.

The God of Vengeance begins to consider His own Passion: the
new tenderness of His Vision of His own Creation demands it.
So Agappy can sing: 'I too have shared dinner in Eden.' Love,
not Death, is in this Arcadia: because the God who created it
will now reveal Himself as a God, not of Death, but of Love.

Mr Warner's plays are often structured around the expression
in a lyrical climax mid-way through the drama of an optimism
which is then qualified. So, in *Meeting Ends* we must wait until
it does before we know whether they are. Act II predictably re-
introduces us to a humanity obsessed with sex and remarkably
godless. When Wrasse cries 'Oh Jesus wept!' she is complaining
about her period pains. Ensoff can thus re-enter as a God of
Wrath. The central image of the trilogy opens his tirade: 'I will
search out Edinburgh (*Or wherever play is being performed*) with
candles, and trample my fury through their houses . . . They
will lie down in the evening and tear their own cheeks from their
faces.' He is outraged by Shango's cynicism: 'Is virtue only self-
interest?' His prayer is ruthless in its logic, logical in its ruthless-
ness: 'Help me not to tolerate what I despise.' Agappy, as
before, argues with him: 'I was never a good hater .. In all my

guilt remember my innocency.' This is in fact Ensoff's Garden of Gethsemane. He is grim; he is 'thinking of his coming agony'. He will accept his Passion: but his purpose remains obscure. 'Only the human remains', he concludes; and 'The dead shall be razed . . . to the ground'. Does this affirm the Resurrection, the Last Judgement, or Annihilation?

Ensoff has certainly become a Christ figure. 'It's an unknown God who's come. If you love him, stay with him', he tells us. Callisterne thinks of him 'as a father'. Shango totally misunderstands Ensoff and acts out of crude fear and envy: he knows not what he does. Ensoff gives the true explanation of his own actions: 'I have seen absence strangle loyalty.' God cannot simply punish sinful Man for disloyalty, since His remoteness partly explains the disloyalty.

Castration is not an outrageous symbol for Crucifixion. It can obviously be linked metaphorically to the Piercing of Christ by the spear which brought forth blood and water, and indeed this incident is sometimes literally interpreted as some form of castration. The same thematic connection is basic to the Myths of the Fisher King and the Wasteland, and runs through the whole Arthurian tradition, as Mr Eliot was able to learn from Miss Weston. Moreover, Ensoff is thus associated with central, but suitably enigmatic, oddball characters in the development of Christian doctrine, Origen and Abelard. Mention of men who were regarded as heretics in their own day leads us to consider the orthodoxy of Mr Warner's theology. How meet, for example, is this ending? It is certainly very curious. Some of the ends hang loose: we never discover what happens to Wrasse or Shango. Perhaps all is well, for the candles are burning now, all six of them. Admittedly, Christ is supposed to walk in the midst of *seven* golden candlesticks; but Mr Warner may be thinking of an altar, where for reasons of symmetry the seventh candle is replaced by a crucifix. Having begun in Genesis, the trilogy ends in Revelation. The trouble is, Ensoff's concluding comments are hardly Christian at all. He tells Callisterne:

> Rest, while the masters of our waking joys
> Rule over us and stretch the oceans' clutch:
> The silent stars play havoc with our toys
> But we have kingdoms that they cannot touch.

The last two lines are crucial: not only did Sir Harold Hobson single them out for comment in his *Sunday Times* review; they are also inscribed on the fireplace in Mr Warner's own rooms in Oxford. Ensoff is human, not divine; and he is faced by a hostile universe. The stars are destructive and silent. There is no music of the spheres here. What then are the 'kingdoms'? Maybe they are kingdoms of the mind, created by love. It is difficult to see how they could be heaven. The moral is less triumph over suffering than patience before it. We are reminded less of Prospero and Miranda than of Lear and Cordelia. The atmosphere is that of:

> As flies to wanton boys, are we to the gods;
> They kill us for their sport.

The play seems to be vacillating between affirming some kind of Christian belief, and achieving a tragic effect. Interestingly, the problem of how to combine these two much concerned Mr Warner's former tutor and colleague, the late Dr T. R. Henn, who wrote both *The Bible as Literature* and *The Harvest of Tragedy*. It is of course quite easy to make Christianity tragic, simply by omitting the Resurrection. There is not much evidence of Resurrection here. The point about Ensoff seems to be precisely that his Passion has made him completely human. Perhaps this is Mr Warner's theory of the Atonement, that the reconciliation of God and Man was achieved by the total separation of Christ from God: he would find support for the idea from several modern theologians, such as Fr Harry Williams. Nevertheless, the Resurrection remains essential to a coherent view of Salvation. The image of the snowdrop breaking through the icy ground in the Epilogue to the play may represent a form of Resurrection, but the imagery is still a little too unspecific. The play ends as Agappy sounds Reveille. Unfortunately, we do not know if anyone answers the call. Of course the audience, already directly addressed in the Epilogue, will rise—from their seats. Unlike Shakespeare, however, we cannot be certain that the globe is any more than a theatre.

The trilogy, then, like *Maquettes*, ends with an appeal. Mr Warner's *Requiem* seems to believe that the dead may rest in peace, but there is some doubt as to whether light perpetual will shine upon them. In terms of the predominate imagery,

Heaven's candles may well be all out. The question remains, why such a theological discussion reaches such an unsatisfactory theological conclusion. However, there have been many non-Christian concepts present in these plays. The hopelessness of *Lying Figures* was almost Manichaean in its belief in the fundamentally dark and irredeemable nature of Man; *Killing Time*, whether Islamic, Nestorian or Monophysite, seemed unable to accept any true integration of God and Man in a crucified Saviour. Any light that did lighten these two plays was Gnostic. *Meeting Ends* transforms the Crucifixion into a tragedy of Renaissance Humanism. What links all these heresies is neo-Platonism. It is worth remembering that one of Mr Warner's major research interests is the neo-Platonism of the Florentine Renaissance. That philosophy has indeed deeply influenced the development of Christian doctrine: the Desert Fathers are a notable example, especially extremist ascetics like St Maron. Nevertheless its fundamental emphasis is on the *distinction* between God and Man, between Heavenly Truth and Earthly Error, between Soul and Body: it cannot really embrace orthodox Incarnation theology. To Greeks, that is foolishness. The conclusion of a neo-Platonist must be the same as the conclusion of Mr Warner's plays: that God may exist; but meanwhile it is necessary to invent Him. The rôle of the biblical quotations now becomes clear: they are not just quotations, but neither is their purpose biblical. The whole purpose and drive of the Bible is towards the affirmation of the Resurrection and Parousia of Christ. Mr Warner's plays are an appeal, against all the evidence, for the Resurrection and Parousia to happen: even so, come, Lord.

William Chapman

No Pink Lampshades: Wit and Humour in the Plays

From his appearance, one would deduce, Mr Warner has to be a writer of drawing-room comedy: the velvet jacket in its viridian sumpture richly reminiscent of the green rooms of a George Alexander or an Allan Aynsworth; the white linen summer suit evocative of strawberries and screaming scarlet puns; the stiff, starched collar gleaming, in these years of disgrace, with only less than Beerbohmesque affectation; the silken tie, suave paradox lurking in its folds, and the elegantly bell-shaped overcoat, eloquent of epigram, all clothe a man of manners to whom one would expect mannered comedy to come quite, quite simply and unnaturally, with all the coy artifice appropriate to such a genre.

Neither are the sartorial details alone suggestive of a wittier and more stylized age. Ostensibly a study (the masquerade assisted by books and a Holy Grail), the backdrop against which the clothes are worn, the man disposed and the plays conceived and written is surely, in its quintessence, a drawing-room, scholarly but sociable. Is it not probable that the kidney-shaped desk would have graced Lady Windermere's writing-room, and might not the tawny keys of the clavichord have been shamed by the whiter fingers of Miss Languish?

Indeed, when he wishes it, and against not only this background but against even the most unpropitious, Mr Warner can transform all life into drawing-room comedy. He allots his companions rôles, feeds us our lines, and sheathes us in a sparkling carapace of words. No literary source has not been rifled for that allusive conversation, so spontaneously studied and studded with paradox, by which even autumnal evenings in mist-laden, leaf-haunted Oxford are irradiated and which, in its rarity, can only be incongruent among the domestic commonplaces of High Table.

Fragments of this conversation may be found, nostalgically for those of us who have shared it, in his plays. In *Lying Figures*, for example, Epigyne says to Gonad:

> In your public world you tell me you are supreme and noble, firm and decisive. A born committee man, dazzling all, knowing when to charm, to look round the table, make the quick, incisive personal stab, deflate with mock innocent joke, appeal to self-interest of each in turn . . .

To those who have read Shakespeare with Mr Warner the passage will prove evocative, since it is his comment, almost verbatim, on the speeches and performance of Troilus in the second scene of Act II of *Troilus and Cressida*, during the war council of the Trojans. That Troilus, the hero and lover of myth, should be seen as the ideal committee man is a nice conceit. Mr Warner's voice may be heard more obliquely in 'If intentions were the criterion of excellence, every sermon would be a masterpiece' or in the warning 'You end up like an Englishman in America, outclassing the classless'. When Chalone in *Killing Time* says 'Sympathy is innocence', Squaloid's answering word-play is just such a rejoinder as the author himself might have given: 'No. Sympathy is impotence.'

Yet these quasi-epigrammatic, often aphoristic, utterances are not permitted to dominate any of the plays, shaping them into the form of drawing-room comedy as they so easily might. This is the more surprising since Mr Warner has obviously inherited some of the spirit of that master of such comedy, Oscar Wilde, whose ideas and techniques, albeit sea-changed, appear not infrequently in Mr Warner's drama. Sometimes a remark will declare its Wildean descent, as in Mr Warner's 'What's the name of that man who's living with his wife?' (which leads us to perceive a further similarity between the two dramatists, namely, the belief that if a thing is worth saying, it is worth saying twice, for in *Meeting Ends* we find 'I thought she and her husband were having an affair'). Wilde's remarks to Gide towards the end of his life are refracted in Agappy's advice 'Don't look for happiness, it only leads to despair', whilst Mr Warner's use of the parable is very similar to that of Wilde's, whose parables on the divine futility of Christ's teachings find a counterpart in Mr Warner's story of God erasing man's faults, only to be disappointed in the man who emerged from the reformation, more perfect indeed but neither so interesting nor so beautiful as before. This idea in turn is a variation on Wilde's theme that it is our vices which endow us with individualism, an idea rehabilitated explicitly in *Troat*:

> Our fallings from perfections, our vices, are what make us individuals; so in the name of common humanity we should cultivate our faults.

It could almost have been said by Lord Henry Wotton or Lord Illingworth—almost, but not quite. For whilst in essence it would have been appropriate to either dandy, it lacks something of the appropriate form. It seems neither sufficiently polished, nor provocative enough in its finality.

This is not at all through any lack of verbal skill on Mr Warner's part; his conversation is enough to assure us of that. But if this is so, why has he chosen not to go that one further step necessary to turn a remark like the above into an epigram perfectly assured, both audacious and orchidaceous? Why are his plays not the drawing-room comedies which his personality and conversation would suggest he is so well fitted to write?

The times are out of joint or, we may assume, are felt to be so by Mr Warner. No longer born, or at any rate bred, in a handbag, men are born over the grave; in the case of Gonad's son, still-born into a grave. The cradle is also the coffin. In Act II of *Killing Time* Squaloid describes his experience at the end of the Second World War, (an experience which the stage setting of a human brain makes more universal by its suggestion of innate cruelty in all human kind):

> When we reached Belsen . . . I soon learned not to waste time with the old or any with typhoid. Only the young, only those we had a chance of saving . . . When I tried to use a needle intravenously, the poor devils wouldn't let me and yelled out 'Nicht Krematorium! Nicht Krematorium!' The Deutsch had been injecting them with paraffin so they'd burn better. (*Pause*) The Nazis have come and gone.

To which Chalone replies:

> And the memory remains.

Burdened by that memory, and all that it symbolizes of man's newfoundland of cruelty, the effect of which on literature George Steiner has analysed so eloquently, was drawing-room comedy ever an option available to Mr Warner, for all his verbal skill and delight in form and other qualifications? This is not to say that a drawing-room comedy could not be written by any-one at all post-1945, only that it could not be written by Mr Warner, with the preoccupations peculiar to him.

But do these preoccupations forbid the plays from being comedies of any sort? Mr Warner himself gives us the yardstick with which to assess them. In the grimmest play, with a pleasing irony, the audience is lectured on comedy. Chalone in *Killing Time*, lecturing on the construction of the brain, talks of the 'seven nerves of the cortex':

> First, climbing fibres for comedy; second, mossy fibres for tra-gedy. As tragedy is the higher mode, the mossy fibres stimu-late the largest number of cells and provoke negative feedback. Comedy on the other hand reasserts balance and peace . . .

Or, to borrow a favourite formulation of Mr Warner's, all comedy ends in wedding.

It is true that all these plays end, if not with a marriage, at least with some sort of reconciliation—but reconciliations so qualified as to be almost more poignant than a clean break, a straightforward separation, and so fatally flawed as to contain, perhaps, the seeds of future dissolution. In the penultimate scene of *Emblems* the two brides embrace and kiss—but what of the bridegroom, left isolated at the end, with only the thrush's song with its suggestion of life to console him? (Yet even that consolation is a dubious one, since 'What contortion leaps the . . . thrush's . . . throat?' suggests a strangled cry as much as a song.) In *Troat* Man and Young Woman finally embrace, only to have, quite literally, coals of fire heaped on their heads. In *Lumen*, Actor and Actress have the will to unite—but are sitting just so far apart that 'their fingertips are not quite able to touch'; at the end of *Lying Figures* Laz and Saph chant to each other a lyrical poem about the union of two lovers:

> Your beauty overwhelmed numb caution's fear;
> Give me the penalty such wrong incurs:
> Prison me in your arms, condemn to stay
> Now I am in and not a hedgehog stirs.

Ah sweet unwise, so strong to take your own possession
Gentle me till the furthest star spills our confession.

—but let us not forget that the speakers are corpses and that the
poem is also about parting. After the same play's depiction of
their fractured marriage, Epigyne and Gonad seem to achieve a
reunion—but a reunion achieved only over the razor-slit body
of Xyster, indeed through the very act of cutting her apart,
whilst the comradeship of Squaloid and Chalone at the end of
Killing Time is expressed in the joint hoisting up of two bodies.
The first of the maquettes began with a parody of marriage—
is it surprising, then, that in *Meeting Ends*, final play of the
trilogy, although Ensoff sits with his arm around Callisterne, his
castration in the previous scene has ruled out, if not the marriage
of true minds, any possibility of fulfilling the first of the reasons
for marriage advanced in the Book of Common Prayer? The
stage directions specify that Ensoff and Callisterne 'must not at
any point kiss', as if to emphasize that, with the end of the
trilogy, harmony can never now be fully achieved, the discords
never finally resolved.

Imperfectly harmonious, these plays can hardly be classed as
comedies; nevertheless, wit and humour persist in them, colour-
ing the whole trilogy, although the colours they add do not
always relieve, but often darken, their already sombre hues.
For, paradoxically, the wit gains much of its peculiar power
from the very atmosphere which forbids us to class the plays as
comedies—the horror (often equal to that of a Jacobean tragedy)
of the murders, torture, incest, castration, blinding and psycho-
logical violence in a strange way informs the wit and humour;
it becomes rather like hearing a death's head laugh.

Like his reconciliations, Mr Warner's humour is marked by
its ambivalence. Inextricably bound up with the plays' serious
themes and frequent horror, which respectively it expresses and
heightens, the wit is inevitably double-edged in its effect. Like
corrosive acid, the humour etches more deeply into the plays a
pattern of tension and horror, and scores more starkly their
themes.

The burden of this austere achievement rests largely upon a
form now generally regarded as expressive of the weakest
humour, or at best as a harmless ingredient of party games: the

pun. To this much debased figure Mr Warner restores a sombre, metaphysical splendour and significance. When George Herbert entitled one of his poems 'The Collar' he was not trying to be feebly humorous, but putting a serious point ingeniously and economically. In this Mr Warner resembles him (and, further, in that, like Herbert in this case, Mr Warner sometimes makes both a theological and an emotional point simultaneously). Mr Warner's puns are often a form of more or less humorous shorthand for the plays' serious themes: the very titles are punning sketches of what is to come, brief overtures in which lurk the embryos of themes to be developed in the main piece. *Lying Figures* concerns figures lying to each other about whom they have lain with; *Killing Time* is a play about a murderous era, impregnated with the boredom and violence that arise from having time to kill (in both senses); *Meeting Ends* is complex with simultaneous suggestions of harmony and disharmony (ragged ends meet, yet perhaps something is ended with a meeting), sexual implications, and the hint that such a play is a meet, fitting end for the trilogy and, perhaps, for humanity.

This use of the pun or other sorts of word-play continues throughout the plays, creating little explosions of multiple meaning which alert the reader to the main themes. Like Very lights, puns explode in multifarious directions, illuminating simultaneously different features of the same ground. One of the most important of these themes is the fragility of the relationship between man and his fellow men, man and his fellow women, and the part that sexuality plays therein. Put like that, it sounds trite and obvious; but in fact many dark and unexpected (indeed unwelcome) places are explored—and it is very often the pun which is the means of exploration. The theme is announced in a punning quotation from, one imagines, that most unpunning of prophets, Job: 'Yet in my flesh shall I see God' (quoted as the epigraph to *Meeting Ends*). It is the predicament of the plays in essence: does man make his flesh a god over him, or is he made in the image of God? Does man see a god in his risen and erected flesh, or the risen God latent in him? And if man's flesh *is* his god, what sort of a god has he summoned up? Life-giving or death-dealing, redemptive or satanic? Appropriately, puns suggest some possible answers to a question implied by a pun:

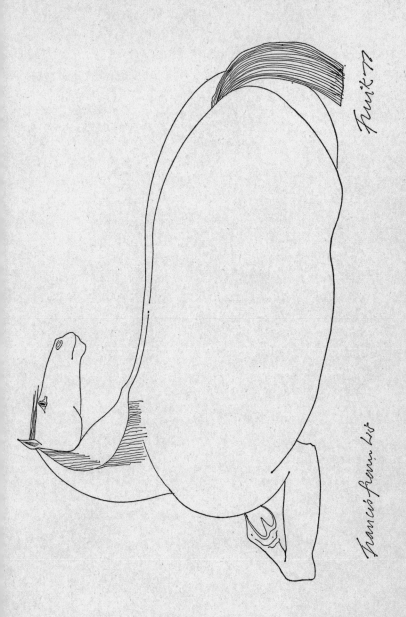

Francis Ferri Lit   Ferri '77

AGAPPY: . . . I once knew a virginal man who had cervical cancer.

WRASSE: He must have been feeling low.

AGAPPY: The crack of doom.

In this formulation the vulva becomes either the entrance to Hades itself, or at least the last trump calling one to judgement which may result in exile to Hades; possibly it becomes the judgement seat itself. Or an answer is suggested by Agappy's request, uniting another theme important to Mr Warner, death, with that of sexuality: 'May I fumble with your dust?'

The problems of our sexuality and our emotions and the moulds we create for them are explored with a complex brevity that would be impossible without word-play. A whole network of possible adulterous relationships is instantly and ominously evoked by Epigyne's and Gonad's exchange:

EPIGYNE: (*Floods of tears*) I always wanted to be a brides-maid; and I'm only a bride!

GONAD: Now come on dear, the best man doesn't always win. That's the point of the wedding ceremony.

But who is the *best* man, and if the husband isn't, will the bride choose a better man later? If the conflict of the sex war is only latent in that quotation, it is encapsulated implicitly in the two puns of Wrasse's definition of marriage as 'Forced labour and endless penal servitude', whilst even such a seemingly trivial piece of word-play as that spoken to Quark whose shoulder-strap has slipped, 'Mind your booby trap', contributes to the swelling theme. Play, when it is Warnerian word-play, has a job of work to do.

This verbal skill, which would have made him an outstanding writer of *vers de société* or drawing-room comedy in an earlier day, is that which, paradoxically, underlines the fact that this comedy is not of manners—but is impelled by a moral concern. One of Wilde's reasons for resorting to the West End for subject-matter was that there men went masked, and in masks lay his chief fascination—in Mr Warner's plays the process of being stripped to the bone is paramount.

> The silent stars play havoc with our toys
> But we have kingdoms that they cannot touch,

proclaims Ensoff in *Meeting Ends*. But the playwright, and by his grace the audience, is more powerful than any planet, and probes and dissects and explores until he lays bare the brain's core, as *Killing Time* reminds us with its great model of a human brain as a stage setting. To expose the 'raw wound of the mind' is Mr Warner's skill, and for this delicate purpose what sharper scalpel than the pun, which erects its own mask only to strip it away, which simultaneously states one meaning and undercuts it with another?

Quite properly, this central moral concern of the trilogy is expressed in a pun in the very first full-length play, *Lying Figures*, when Gonad says 'My mind is still, as yet, undefaced', to which Epigyne replies 'We'll soon fix that', proceeding to fulfil the sinister implications of her words by stripping layer after layer from their marital relationship, defacing its façade and Gonad's portrait of himself as a husband, telling him that their baby is not his, of her desire to leave, of her inevitable lovers. The workings of her mind, and their past intimate relations are exposed by puns—the camouflage ripped away from the trip wires which make an ambush of their relationship and fill the space between them. Mockingly, Epigyne reads out a letter which Gonad once wrote:

> 'You are indeed my pearl of great prize.'
> Prize? Shouldn't it be 'price'?

Even while restoring the quotation she hints at her sense of being a chattel—yet perhaps too at a secret satisfaction that, through her adultery, she is at least a chattel bought at a high price. A little earlier, word-play has discovered another trap:

GONAD: You weave a net of malice out of the threads of goodness.
EPIGYNE: Threats?
GONAD: *Threads!*

The pun is able to perceive and suggest subterranean movements in the mind which may not be discernible on its surface. Gonad says he is not yet defaced—the fate predicted by Ensoff for the widows of Edinburgh, who will 'lie down . . . and tear their own cheeks from their faces'. It is this outrage that the oh so innocuous and witty pun metaphorically achieves. How close is comedy to tragedy in Mr Warner's plays!

Certainly the laughter is implected with pain—we are reminded of the city that died of laughing. The humour is rooted in a bitter soil, as in, for example, the comic gardening scene in Act 3 of *Lying Figures*, when Epigyne orders Gonad to do something about the garden, and in which the raking, the rolling, the spiking of the lawn are carried out by Gonad in speeded-up motion, the effect of an old film reinforced by his striped Edwardian bathing costume, 'such as are worn in comic seaside postcards'. Yet the scene is placed in a bitter context (Gonad's and Epigyne's argument), it ends in near-violence (Gonad's menacing gestures with the shears), and it springs from bitterness; when, just after this scene, we reach Epigyne's lines:

> The only person who can do anything to hurt me emotionally is you . . .
> Only you have bitten into me like corrosive acid

we see the source from which all the preceding 'comic' action arose—the pain of the raw wound of Epigyne's mind has impelled the comedy which, seen down this perspective, takes on a new significance.

Pain and laughter are intertwined, too, in Wrasse's speech in *Meeting Ends* when she recounts the genesis of her unfortunate first marriage:

> So I married! Though I didn't lead him on. I'd no idea he had it in his head when he proposed. How could I tell him? Said I wanted time to think. How could I say 'No' without hurting? Should I *type* an answer? Would have to practise, and anyway, too long delay would be cruel, his best years would have gone, so finally I said 'Yes', but didn't, and got pregnant as a result.

Yet this pleasantly nonsensical account is of a marriage that eventually drove her husband into a lunatic asylum, where he 'asks whether he's keeping my grave as I like it when I visit him'.

Sometimes the humour becomes so loaded with pain that no laughter is possible. The word-play turns deadly serious when Xyster in *Lying Figures*, about to be strung up and cut open, is

admonished by Gonad 'Be calm, dear' and she replies 'I am . . .
becalmed'. Laughter is precluded, but the pathos is all the more
intense, the starkness of the word-play all the more sudden, for
the memories of the laughter that so many happier examples of
word-play have so often provoked.

This subversive use of humour is Mr Warner's way of generat-
ing unease, of implicating the audience. We laugh at Gonad's
comic garden turn, and then realize that we have been laughing,
albeit obliquely, at Epigyne's lacerated feelings. More drastic-
ally affecting our view of the whole play and of our reaction to it,
is the scene in which the naked Xyster, inverted, is presumed to
be sliced open by Gonad's razor—uniting the themes of death
and love, sexuality and cruelty, in one visible pun; individual
verbal puns had been compacted of some of these various
elements, but this scene unites and takes up all the puns we have
laughed at during the play. And, as a result, it immediately
wrenches all those past puns into a new context—the past
laughter now echoes mockingly in our ears when we see the
culmination of much that we have been laughing at. Our
laughter is qualified in retrospect; we stand condemned.

Indeed, is this not proper? Let us remember the title of the
trilogy as a whole. Laughter at a *Requiem*? Such is the proposi-
tion that accuses us if we accept, as we must, the presence of wit
and humour, however ambivalent, in Mr Warner's plays. A
bride's mother may weep at a wedding (and what more fitting
reaction to the marriages which Mr Warner celebrates), but
invert the paradox—and who may laugh at a requiem? Yet in
Requiem we not only laugh during the service, we laugh at the
corpse whose soul we are, perhaps, commemorating. A positive
coruscation of puns cascades from the gums of Laz and Saph:

LAZ: I'm glad you're awake. Do you feel putrid?
         Sapph rallies and sits up.
SAPPH: I may be corrupting, but I have certain standards.

or

SAPPH: It's dispiriting in the refrigerator.
LAZ: Cold as summer.
SAPPH: What did my chemist used to say? 'We keep your
         life in our fridge.'
LAZ: Very potent of him.

SAPPH: Let's pretend we are able . . .

LAZ: Why bother? All my life I've been dying for this.

SAPPH: (*Stung*) Oh all right! (*Pause*) It's not vital.

LAZ: (*Humbled*) I'm mortified.

SAPPH: (*Brightening*) I'm not sanguine about our chances.

The puns gain point when we realize that they are spoken not by elegantly over-dressed young people, artificial, perhaps, but alive, as even Maugham's are, but by two dead bodies in a mortuary (presumably trying to corpse one another). The skull splits, the flesh peels, the jaw drops, and a jest, sparkling among the decrepitude, hard and gem-like amidst decomposition, flashes forth. It is a derangement of our accepted notions, and, as a result, all highly disconcerting. That comedy, one of whose definitions is its healing power, should in *Requiem* be used to dislocate our expectations is very Warnerian.

This unsettling quality of his humour is seen reflected in his amusing yet discomforting analysis of cliché. A cliché reassures us, soothing us with a sense of places known: it is a word or words covered with moss and undergrowth, the sharp edges blurred, strenuous contours no longer distinct.

Mr Warner's humour strips away these accretions so that the comforting forms of words taken for granted no longer hedge us in:

OLD MAN: The road is out of order. That is why the notice says *Road Works*.

YOUNG MAN: Because it doesn't?

Although it comes from an old nightwatchman, there are none the less overtones of Alice (incidentally emphasizing how that most proper little girl was one of the most subversive Victorian characters) in the rigidly logical and literal way in which an over-worked phrase is questioned: the young man patiently explains, 'I don't think you see what I'm saying.' 'See?' says the night-watchman. 'Don't you mean hear?' These are trivial, in a way, yet this corrosion of linguistic preconceptions underscores the plays' moral questioning of other sorts of preconceptions. Indeed, there is no need to separate the two: a concern with language can be simultaneously moral and linguistic. Sinister implications of our loose and sloppy catch-phrasing are extracted by Mr Warner's deft pen: when Gonad says 'It's the innocent that suffer', Guppy is quite logical to draw the conclusion that 'The only way to avoid suffering is to be guilty'. But, of course, when we use Gonad's phrase we don't mean to imply the wide-boy conclusion of Guppy (who at least treats the language with respect, however)—yet it seems that cliché breeds evil, and that when we make words loose living, we imply the actual committal of a sin. As Lewis Carroll wrote, in a letter about *The Hunting of the Snark*, 'Words mean more than we mean to express when we use them.'

Nor is this exploration of cliché trivial when viewed from another angle. That which makes us ill at ease in one context, in another is a source of reassurance. For Mr Warner's exposure of cliché signals his concern that words should not 'slip, slide, perish, Decay with imprecision', his concern that the language should have meaning. And this is important, in one context in particular.

The plays are permeated more thoroughly with one question than with any other: are we Absurd?

> . . . for man to be true?
> Reason rejects such lunacy run rife

are among the opening lines of *Meeting Ends*. Indeed, sometimes it seems hardly worth asking the question, so often comes the answer, accepted as an accomplished fact, that we are truly hopeless, futile and without future:

> If humanity is a race then the game is lost, the future has run out

(again the pun, announcing the grand theme). As Laz, the male corpse, says, 'We can't think in terms of the future any more', which may or may not be reasonable for a corpse to state, but might it not, asks Mr Warner, be horribly appropriate even for those of us still alive? Indeed, are we alive in any significant sense? 'At best we are worthless.' Do we inhabit a universe that has any reference to us at all?

> Emptiness enfolds. Darkness encroaches on the light, and in lightness we dare not comprehend.

'Is a short, ecstatic life preferable to a long, dull one?' asks Epigyne, to which Gonad replies: 'Neither makes sense in the

long perspective.' Like a threnody, the claims of our nullity
weave in and out of the plays, haunting the words and action,
infecting and shaping every situation. Almost overpowering as
the statements are, however, there is still an option in the plays
to question them. But how resolve the problem—absurd or not?
Mr Warner's use of comedy perhaps points us to an answer to
this serious question.

Until recently the axiom was universally accepted that our
power over words uniquely distinguished us from the animals;
indeed, it still has much force. One of Mr Warner's characters,
however, advances the idea that it is our capacity for suicide
that marks us out from the beasts. If we, our human selves,
possess meaning, then our words will have meaning; if, on the
other hand, we have no meaning it will not matter much what
sounds or shapes our words take, and suicide will be far more
expressive of our apprehension of our predicament, a far more
effective response to it, than our now meaningless words could
be. The clue, then, to Mr Warner's answer to his question is to
be found in his estimation of words. Once again, word-play
points the crux: 'What are your words worth?' says Agappy to
the Chancellor in *Meeting Ends*. What are Mr Warner's words
worth? Is he so gripped by the pain of man's absurdity that he
sees language as Shango, pain-racked, sees it: 'a drunken king
on holiday, swaggering and strutting . . .' ('full of sound and
fury, signifying nothing')? Or does it have some significance for
him? How seriously does he take our capacity for suicide, and
how seriously our capacity to make and use a language that is
expressive and capable of meaning?

It is significant that in posing the very question which, if
answered, would solve the riddle of Absurdity, Mr Warner
invokes a classic poet, for Mr Warner's use of poetry in his plays
points us to an understanding of the function of his comedy.
Poetry has inspired many fine sentiments, from Aristotle, inscrib-
ing in the *Poetics*, 'Poetry is something more philosophic and of
graver import than history', to Keats, scribbling to Reynolds
that 'Poetry . . . should strike the reader as a wording of his own
highest thoughts.' It is no accident that Mr Warner punctuates
his drama with poetry: seen in the resplendent light of these
two quotations it is a protest against the notion that we are
absurd (although, usually in 'archaic' forms, even the poems

contribute to the typical Warnerian complexity, hinting that our conceit of ourselves as immortal, as not absurd, may no longer be viable). Similarly with the humour and the wit. The use of the many-meaninged pun is a protest against the idea that words, and by implication we who use them, have no meaning; the word-play, both in its expression of Mr Warner's sheer delight in words, and in its assertion that words can contain meanings, complex yet precise, hints at the possibility of non-absurd values. With rare tension he deploys the form of his words to argue against their intellectual content: much of the argument they express concerns, directly or indirectly, the possibility of our absurdity—but their rich expression of that same argument partially refutes the possibility. His delight in words implies his belief in them and his disbelief that suicide is the only thing that distinguishes us from the beasts. Even such a trivial pun as 'she married . . . into the nubility' is connected to this central impulse and is thereby rendered more electric, more vigorous. Thus is Mr Warner's humour indicative of his high seriousness.

That no such question of Absurdity troubles the polished surface of drawing-room comedy helps to explain the absence of pink lampshades and epigrams from Mr Warner's plays. Certainty is needed for the deployment of epigram—a certainty for the epigram to invert and an audacious certainty on the part of the epigrammatist that in inverting it he is right. An epigram expresses an often insolent finality and assurance which Mr Warner would not hope to achieve; the pun, the ambiguous word-play, is more suited to a dramatist still groping for answers, still exploring. A pun throws out numbers of meanings, all of them possible routes for the explorer to follow—routes, indeed, into problems which other puns have often by their complexity evoked, for Mr Warner's wit is impregnated with sombre themes (themes which, none the less, when revolved, throw off such glittering linguistic sparks). Mr Warner's wit is unlike that of the drawing-room dramatists twice over. Not only is it an exploratory voyage, it can only suggest the destination.

8

Evie Garratt

Working with Warner

The power and the poetry leapt from the typescript. It was moving, dazzling; often incomprehensible. It was *Lying Figures* by Francis Warner—a name then unknown to me. 'I can't understand everything he's getting at,' I thought, 'but this man certainly can write—I do believe he's a bit of a genius.'

And after having been in all three plays of the Warner trilogy, and having come to know, not only his work, but also the man himself, as author, director, and friend, I still think the same. If genius is an extra large supply of the life force allied to originality of vision and a virtuoso's mastery of the English language, then Francis Warner has a better right to that title than many. Philosophy, mythology, zoology, astronomy, gynaecology, physics, mathematics, music, and art—he is fascinated by them all, and uses his knowledge of them all in his plays. He is equally interested in the vagaries of human behaviour—and is not above indulging in a good old gossip. His conversation, like his writing, is punctuated by puns, highlighted by humour and accented by arcane allusions: it's laced with lyricism, spiced with sex—and he likes alliteration too.

His understanding of women is almost frightening. He respects their strengths while despising their weaknesses. In his company a woman feels wiser, wittier, more accomplished, and more attractive than she really is; so naturally women seek his company.

As a director, he is for the most part gentle and self-effacing, but he can also be utterly ruthless. He will jump on you if you depart from the script by as much as a syllable—yet he will leave you virtually free to create your own interpretation of an entire rôle. In Agappy's complex and beautifully written solo scene in *Meeting Ends* (Agappy, incidentally, was created with me in mind) he gave only three directions: two were purely technical, and the third was that a particular pause should be considerably shortened (he was absolutely right).

For the actor Francis's plays are a joy, but they are also a tremendous challenge. They have no straight-through line of plot, the text is full of apparent non-sequiturs, and the characters change not only from scene to scene, but also sometimes from line to line. One moment you are rattling off schoolboy puns, the next you are speaking the most exquisite poetry. You have to use every note in your vocal range, you have to be mentally alert and physically fluid, and lightning fast with your costume changes. A Warner play stretches the actor to the full; —often literally. In the course of the trilogy I have been hung up on a meat hook, I have stridden the stage on stilts and ridden a hobby-donkey (!) with heavy crutches on my back, my arm muscles have been developed hurling the net of a retiarius, and my stomach muscles have been hardened by being sat upon by a hefty six-footer.

Yes, Francis demands a great deal from his actors, but nothing he can't or doesn't do himself. He plays the harpsichord well, he's a dab hand at the drums, and he can even produce a recognizable tune on the trumpet. At rehearsals he showed a child-like enthusiasm for having a go on the stilts, for mastering the pogo stick (happily not my problem), for swinging on the crutches. Though slight of physique, he is physically brave to the point of recklessness—and his energy is inexhaustible. He will stay up all night setting the lighting and then rehearse all next day without a sign of weariness. Yet he suffers from crippling migraines, from which experience he distilled the powerful speech portraying pain in *Meeting Ends*—a speech the actor, typically, delivers while spread-eagled naked in a precariously balanced wheel.

But if Francis asks a great deal from his actors, he gives them much in return. He has the utmost confidence in his cast and is always generous, particularly with his praise. Indeed, sometimes he can be over-confident, for Warner is the supreme optimist—the arch exponent of 'it-will-be-all-right-on-the night', which maddeningly enough, it usually is! He enjoys exercising a benevolent paternalism over his cast, and cherishes the romantic illusion that they are one big happy family (and here again, they often are). In Edinburgh he rents a house which we all share (another example of his generosity—the accommodation is 'thrown in')[1] and when he can, Francis shares it with us. In a domestic setting, as at work, he is always cheerful, even at breakfast. He runs a broken-down car, and regularly gives those of us without transport lifts to the theatre. A nerve-racking kindness this—for as a driver he displays that same bland disregard for obstacles that he does in other areas of his life. And who but Francis would lodge himself and his cast in a house with the name of the landlord, Macbeth, writ large on the door?—a name from which lesser theatrical mortals would flee in superstitious terror. But whether this springs from a bravery that defies the gods, a Puckish sense of humour, or sheer ignorance of a theatrical tradition it is difficult to tell. In this, as with all Francis's actions, you can never be sure of the underlying motive. He is as ambiguous and multifaceted as any of the characters in his plays, and like his plays, he defies logical analysis. He is a lovable tyrant, a shy publicity-seeker, a simple sophisticate, a childish sage; he can be the endearing amateur or the cold professional.

He writes his plays at speed, often only completing them at the last possible moment (though he may have carried them in his head for months, even years)—and when necessary, he can write to order. During rehearsals of *Meeting Ends* he suddenly realized that Agappy needed a change-of-mood speech before Ensoff's entrance. 'Give me two minutes, Evie,' he said. He sat down in the stalls and after exactly two minutes he handed me a page torn from his notebook on which he'd scribbled the following:

> When the shades lengthen and the evening comes, and the busy world is hushed, then let me lighten my heart for the last time, sort my thoughts out of their wrong stockings, turn over the alarm-clock, and wander my allotment's end. Come, little ones; we have the washing-up to cook, breakfast in heaven, and the light of the grave. Weep your wisdom with wonder and wander wide over the world, for weariness wins.

I copied this lovely evocation of the evening of life into my working script and it went into the published version without alteration. And yet that same man, who could produce such

[1] With husbands, wives, children, and pets accommodated too!

gem-like prose in less time than it takes to boil an egg, often has no sense of time whatsoever—or of priorities. For instance, only four days before the opening of *Killing Time*, when the cast needed every moment to perfect their rôles, he spent nine hours of valuable rehearsal time on a photo call. Another irritant to his actors, though it has its funny side too, is his habit of giving you the explanation of an involved line as if he had it in mind before he wrote it, when you're 99% sure he's just thought it up that very minute.

Like all creative artists, Francis is a snapper-up of the happy accident. At the first dress rehearsal of *Meeting Ends*, when something had to be found to support the bean-sticks which are dressed to become a scarecrow, one of the technical staff produced a scarlet fire-bucket. Warner the director found it good; it was used in performance, and subsequently became part of the published stage directions.

I strongly suspect that if someone had asked Warner the author 'Why a fire-bucket?' he would have replied 'Well, it's obvious. The crossed bean-sticks are a crucifix. They represent the spiritual. The sand in the bucket represents the earth, the physical, and the "Fire" on the bucket is of course the fires of hell.'

But perhaps his most maddening trait (and one which really hurts his admirers because it harms him) is his obstinate refusal to adapt his bizarre and cumbersome stage properties to the practical limitations of his theatre. If Warner the designer wants a giant representation of a human brain, or a heavy working guillotine (as in *Killing Time*), or (as in *Lying Figures*) an unwieldy full-sized tree in the shape of a vulva, then have them he must—disregarding lack of wing space, paucity of stage hands, and seemingly interminable waits between scenes.

Yes, working in Warnerland is not always bliss—at rehearsals one swings between exhilaration and depression, between satisfaction and near-despair. But looking back one forgets the pangs and remembers only the pleasure; so that if asked what it's like to be in a Warner play, one finds onself saying 'Great', a term that could equally well be used to describe Francis himself.

But oh, how I wish I could see the Warner trilogy presented after really adequate rehearsal time, on a revolving stage, with a designer who would translate the author's extraordinary visual images into workable properties to ensure a smooth and fast-flowing production. If this were to happen, then the effect would be so overwhelming that at once Francis Warner would achieve the universal acclaim for his unique contribution to modern drama that he so truly merits.

I said I wish I could see this, but of course I don't mean it literally; for to 'see' as opposed to 'being in' the Warner trilogy, would deprive me of the repetition of one of the most stimulating and rewarding experiences of my theatrical life—a painful privilege and an exhausting honour for which I shall always be grateful.

9

Tim Prentki

Requiem for the Living

The fundamental structural principle of Francis Warner's theatre is paradox. Death breeds life, war friendship, marriage adultery. The puns of the plays' titles should prepare us. *Lying Figures* combines the posture of death with that of copulation and *Meeting Ends* repeats the associations. With each orgasm we die a little more—the Elizabethans used 'to die' in both senses—and Mr Warner's drama is at the centre organic; the middle is not excluded. The prevailing themes of the three plays are death, war and sex. But these themes cannot be neatly extrapolated from the text and traced through a play, for each theme is described in terms of the other two. Thus war and sex lead alike to death; sex is seen as a battle terminating in the destruction of one party and war, though resulting in death, can be maintained by virtue of the next generation whose presence is guaranteed by sex.

The *Maquettes* are models for the longer works that follow, though each one encompasses all the main themes of the major plays. *Emblems*, like its parent play *Lying Figures*, has a wedding and a skeleton but Bride Two is a victim of the 'menstrual clock', like Wrasse in *Meeting Ends*. *Troat* is what the Old Man sees in the fire just as *Killing Time* is set inside the human brain, but Venus' Mousetrap referred to in this maquette is to recur in concrete form in *Meeting Ends*. Many images which dominate the double trilogy unite in the sides of meat of *Lumen*, which not only prepare us for the title of the parent play *Meeting Ends* but also the two slabs of meat that Xyster will become after she has been split down the centre, and the dead bodies of Kuru and Phagocyte strung up like meat during the final scene of *Killing Time*. Already it is clear that a developmental approach to these plays is futile, for the images are not stretched out in a convenient line but are overlaid to produce an effect of gathering complexity. Once inside the Warner playhouse our watches stop

('Time is only space in the head'), start again of their own volition, move round at their own speed and finally go backwards. As the central play's title implies, Time is both active and passive, the agent of destruction and the thing destroyed.

The opening of *Emblems* introduces the element of contradiction which represents paradox made manifest. Though dark it is light and rain accompanies the sunshine. The spirit of contradiction carries over into the speech of the two brides, and haunts these plays with an insistence comparable to the theatre of Ionesco. Conventional expectations, this time associated with the marriage ceremony, are aroused only to be deflated as Oscar Wilde's adage is enacted:

In married life three is company and two is none.

The triangular relationship in Mr Warner's theatre is to be the dominant one. He thrives on triangles; here Bride One, Bride Two and Groom; later Gonad, Epigyne and Guppy; finally Wrasse, Shango and Callisterne. Analysing one theme in terms of two others is reflected in each character's need to define himself in terms of two others. There is no residue of the classical personality, just a series of rôles to be played. The survivors are those who can play the greatest number convincingly, as Chalone demonstrates most strikingly at the climax of *Killing Time*. Each bride expresses this desire while exposing the limitations of which marriage in Mr Warner's theatre must beware:

BRIDE ONE: I wanted to be his mistress as well as his wife.
BRIDE TWO: And I his bride as well as his whore.

The essence of Harold Pinter's play *The Lover* is encapsulated in these lines. Where society is at its most ceremonial and therefore most pompous, Mr Warner is ready to probe beneath the surface:

BRIDE TWO: He asked me to envelop whoredom with ceremony.

Bride Two recreates the experience of waiting for her lover, a situation which is worked out again in Epigyne's monologue to kill time before Guppy's appearance and in Wrasse's before the arrival of Shango. The triangle again dominates and the woman is seen playing different rôles as mistress and wife. The similarities are not confined to structure since all three women are also predators by nature; trappers of men and dominators of women. Bride Two's 'snap' is the sound made by Venus' Mousetrap as it is sprung by Wrasse on Shango or the noise of the lover's head being bitten off by the female preying mantis, Epigyne. The dominance over women is depicted in images of masculinity, the most sudden being Bride Two's change of costume, though the more complete is the ability of the wrasse to change sex. The dark glasses ('the light is dark') link Bride Two with Epigyne. The dominant-subservient female pairing is a leitmotif of the trilogy; Bride One and Bride Two; Xyster and Epigyne; Quark and Kuru; Callisterne and Wrasse. Their differing fates reflect the changes in mood as the cycle revolves. Xyster is Epigyne's victim while Quark and Kuru are both taken by the war, whereas Callisterne and Wrasse achieve a type of emotional fulfilment appropriate to their desires.

The most powerful image of *Emblems* carries the central paradox of *Requiem*. In the midst of life we are in death and yet because the experience can be formulated in words its opposite is equally plausible. In the midst of death we are in life. Though no image can be located to set against the skeleton on the swing or the infant skeleton of *Lying Figures*, the last words of *Emblems* ensure that both ends of the paradox are met:

Yet what contortion leaps the . . . thrush's . . . throat?

The short step from 'throat' to *Troat* confronts us with the gratuitous killing of the mouse by the Old Man, his army great-coat suggesting he was trained for the job. Chalone's opening speech in *Killing Time* reminds us that 'man and the fox are deformed' by their appetite for murder and that 'war' (like sex) 'is a fever in our brain'. The fox can at least moderate its sexual demands:

The silver fox is on heat only eight days a year. And those are in February.

The two drives are closely linked and both figure strongly in the Old Man's obsessions, for his brazier contains both the flames of war's destruction and the fires of lust. If the themes belong predominantly to *Killing Time*, the verbal echoes are with *Meeting Ends*:

> I am an old man staring at the coals,
> Seeking sensations while the brain runs rife.
> Staring through eyes that swoop on beasts in holes.
> Inhabit each last strangled cry for life.
> Companion thoughts; protean, unconfined.
> The spawning cancers of a dying mind.

Ensoff is to rework the image:

> . . . and for man to be true?
> Reason rejects such lunacy run rife.

But if there is a foreshadowing of his comforting of Callisterne in the Woman's 'snuggle' up to Old Man, the similarity is more apparent than real. For while Ensoff maintains a distance from his creation for all but one moment, the author made flesh, a distance achieved by his transcendence of passion, the Old Man uses his imagination to gratify his senses. When gratification is about to be denied he intervenes to destroy his creation. This is very different from Ensoff's divine rage:

> Help me not to tolerate what I despise.

The Old Man is roused by sexual jealousy, another reversal of the expected order since the character nearest death is the one most alive. Though the Old Man is an agent of destruction, yet his words provide the antidote to the skeleton of *Emblems*:

> But isn't it true, a cemetery *is* where the dead live?

Mr Warner writes a requiem for the living because the dead have no need of one. The contrast between the imaginative richness of the dead and the spiritual poverty of the living is fully explored in *Lying Figures*. The Old Man also poses the main thematic problem of that play:

> Because a man lies with a woman once, must he the rest of his life?

A device which is to become a Warner trade-mark is introduced in *Troat*. The moment of intensest lyricism is juxtaposed with the act of fiercest violence. Here lyric precedes the action but the more usual order is the reverse. In *Lumen* violence precedes lyric to be followed by more violence then more lyric.

The castration of Xyster is followed by the poem of Sapphira
and Laz; the mock execution of Quark gives way to the poems
of Quark and Kuru and the dance of Quark. Most moving of
all is Ensoff's lyric affirmation of human capability following
immediately on his own castration. Mr Warner has adapted
this technique from the Japanese Noh plays via Yeats's, both of
which he has studied extensively. In each of the major plays this
juxtaposition provides a focal point for the emotional under-
currents. In a theatre where plot and characterization are of
minimal importance, Mr Warner makes the most of a device
which enables him to confront his surrealist visions with the
classicism of his verbal power.

The themes and structures of the full-length plays are set out
in skeletal form in *Emblems* and *Troat* but *Lumen* introduces us to
the dramatis personae, their changing relationships, even their
vocabulary, existing beneath the dominant image of the hanging
meat. The actor and the actress are able to take on any rôle their
imaginations can create, so Mr Warner gives them a full range
to work on. The actor plays by turns, husband, lover, God,
father, landlord, housewife, bishop, politician, doctor, fish-
monger, also incorporating the speech-idioms of the working
class, besides the rôles which the actress casts him in such as
film-star. She is wife, tart, mother and bread-winner. They are
like slabs of meat, distinguished from each other only by their
sex organs, on which the dramatist can write whatever he
wants. On this stage everything is real of which the imagination
can conceive and since all human life is rôle-play the permuta-
tions are infinite. The situation, not the character, dictates the
choice of rôle as we see in the relationship between Wrasse and
Shango where the struggle for control changes from scene to
scene. This acting of a part is at its most extreme in *Killing Time*
where Kuru moves from little girl to old woman and Quark the
opposite way in the space of one scene. If you are not as young
as you feel, you can at least be as young as you say. The theatrical
illusion where the actor frequently takes on a part wildly in-
appropriate to his age is exposed not to remind the audience that
they are in a theatre (many other devices are doing that) but
because it is the illusion of life where the allocation of rôles can
be every bit as absurd. *Lumen* demonstrates in an extreme form
the rôle-play which is pervasive in the plays to come. Thus the

speakers need no names, for they can be designated by their function as Actor and Actress. However, they may have something to say to each other which the rôles cannot accommodate; a personal communication beyond the scope of the stereotypes they have eagerly embraced. They stretch out their hands to each other but cannot touch because their words have extinguished meaning:

ACTOR: We have left it too late.
ACTRESS: We shouldn't have joked.
ACTOR: Darken our lightness.
ACTRESS: Bear with our weakness.

Like Nagg and Nell in their dustbins of *Endgame* or Laz and Sapphira in their fridges they recognize their mistake but cannot rectify it. They can only be distinguished apart by their vices: a distinction that the Young Man in *Troat* was the first to point out.

The necessity of playing a part is not the only limitation on human understanding. Our bodies are purposely limited to cherish our hopes:

ACTOR: The infinite variety of the eyeball, when the lid is down, successfully excludes the light. The knee is capped.
ACTRESS: We know so much!
ACTOR: Enough to know how little. Adequate to realize our outrageous inadequacy.
ACTRESS: No dear. That for which we grieve should make us rejoice.
ACTOR: We must seek ever to know more!
ACTRESS: This I speak with tears, our knowledge is curtailed lest we should despair.

The paradox is re-enforced by Sapphira:

We see enough to see how little we can see.

Mankind is condemned to be for ever questing, but too limited to find out. The structure of the brain is built to support this Kafkaesque situation. We could not cope with the capacity for infinite knowledge:

Chalone is the stopping agent that prevents the brain growing too large for its skull.

So Chalone, as the agent of society in *Killing Time*, prevents the individual from growing at the expense of the social good. He is the provider of checks in his multiple restrictive rôle as judge, hangman, priest and army officer. But though he proves indispensable in war conditions, the possibility of transcending the normal human limits, of imagining the unimaginable, is the hope for the future only expressed albeit very tentatively in *Meeting Ends*.

The two instincts most difficult to harness to the needs of the Establishment are the violent and the sexual, but society creates wars to absorb the first and marriage to siphon off the second. These prove successful in holding society together but they both require victims. The destruction of married life is as complete as that of war, as the Actress points out, again taking one theme in terms of another:

The marriage licence is a charter for violation.

The domestic hearth is thus interchangeable with the licensed brothel since the Actress can switch from moment to moment from wife to prostitute. These plays are maquettes, not sketches; small-scale models of the works to come. Thematically there is nothing left out, but what is here just a line or an image is to become a scene or a character in the full-length plays. The brazier becomes the brain, the night watchman the guardian of the planet.

The cold of *Lumen* carries over into the mortuary of *Lying Figures*, where the hanging sides of meat are being stored in the deep freeze. The storage proves to be a restoration at least of the imagination if not of the body. Guppy is to inform us that

The world after death is all back to front. The dead are queers.

But death here is only a mirror-image of life and Sapphira's white funeral will be reflected in Epigyne's black wedding. The funeral is an initiation into a pure state while the wedding is the price to be paid for past sins. As death brings new life in its wake so birth is the passing on of a fatal disease, life:

The way to stop transmission of death is to call a halt to pro-creation.

Laz and Sapphira observe the action of the play but cannot enter into it. They have already passed across the battlefield, have acquired some wisdom, but cannot communicate it. Like the Actor and Actress of *Lumen* they can only replay the rôles of their former life, this time in the knowledge of their unimportance. Gonad provides the structural link between the living and the dead. He works at night like the Old Man of *Troat*, and this places him at one remove from daily life. In explaining his reasons he outlines a typical life:

> Peck on the cornflakes cheek, soaked through at the bus-stop, daily squash each way in the tube, commuters' corset till sixty-five, then pppfft! the six by four.

This summary echoes the compressed boredom invoked by the Actor and Actress in *Lumen*:

> ACTOR: Compliments, date, cinema, chocolates, snog, finger, front-room, row, parents, wedding, brat, a whore, semi-forgiveness, repeat endlessly, death?
>
> ACTRESS: Security, legal aid, grandchildren.
>
> ACTOR: Flesh, words, promise kept under pressure, result —new flesh, words, flesh, word, flesh grows up and then all the fumbling and bumbling all over a-fondling-gain.

Wrasse's mime in *Meeting Ends* is another example of this awareness of just being a component on a circular assembly line that can never be stopped. Gonad has jumped off, but only to land on another one. His wife is now no longer synchronized with his sexual routine:

> Wake him at bedtime so he can go out and do a day's work; while I lie in the dark counting the stars like daisies in the grass.

Epigyne is a woman of conventional desires and aspirations. She wants to exploit what society offers, not seek for alternatives, as her behaviour in Act Three demonstrates. She wants a man who will exert himself around the house and do the gardening.

No matter how exotic their fantasies, these dominating women have very mundane expectations, as an exchange between Shango and Wrasse in the fair-ground reveals:

SHANGO: You'll come to a meet end. What more do you want?
WRASSE: Pieces of scrap iron, springs, bolts, screws, saucepans, the whole rubbish dump.
SHANGO: I really don't like going out with women nowadays. They all have either divorce or marriage at the front of their minds.

But Epigyne gets small comfort from her lover, Guppy. Apart from being unreliable, he belongs to the same night world as Gonad. As an undertaker he stands between the living and the dead, enjoying the paradoxes of both worlds to the full. He is the master of appearance and rôle-play. He makes no distinction between imaginative and concrete reality. As in the selection of lies, he accepts the ones which answer the call of his senses. Like the actor, in the world of rôle-play, his public life, he is supreme:

All undertakers are the same. It's the job. We in our profession are actors. Yes, actors. That would be a good word to describe it.

As we saw in *Lumen* the danger is that he will never escape the confines of his rôle and he provides no evidence that he does escape. But he does at least have the compensation of a double rôle; both rôles suggested in his profession of undertaker. He takes the dead under and is a taker of undies. Like the title *Lying Figures*, he combines death with copulation until the two facts unite in the syphilis which strikes him down.

Epigyne is thwarted by one sort of call of nature while Wrasse is the victim of another. The women's physical make-up puts them in closer touch with the rhythm of nature, specifically the surge of the immortal breakers and the music of the conch.

The scene dissolves suddenly into the tableau to remind the audience how close to the surface of this play the influence of the visual arts is. The title of the play invokes both the permanent bones of Moore's statues and the ephemeral flesh of Bacon's paintings[1], with the nervous frailty of Giacommetti's figures in the background. The figure of the head-covered nude comes directly from Delvaux as the text of *Lying Figures* demonstrates. Though the vividness of his visual images is one of the strength's of Mr Warner's theatre, the influence of the fine arts world seems too direct, almost crude by comparison with the manner in which it is absorbed into the fabric of *Meeting Ends*, most notably this play's fair-ground scene inspired by Kandinsky's 'Painting with Red Spot' (1914). The difference in the later play is enshrined in the inspiration. Whereas the Kandinsky has been engulfed by the writer's imagination to reappear in an original, relevant image, some of the pictorial influences on *Lying Figures* seem to be merely taken over to root as best they can in alien soil.

From the darkness of illicit passion the scene moves to the daylight of domesticity. Epigyne is now in her rôle of wife which involves her in taking the initiative to arouse her husband's interest, an initiative which in turn leads her to adopt a masculine aggressiveness which has the effect of reducing Gonad to an impotence which does not serve her end, he being unwilling to take on the rôle of male preying mantis:

> And the female praying mantis during copulation bites off the head of her love; who, all the same, still continues to thrust away with undiminished fervour. I'm getting tired of you.

However, Gonad's impotence is probably just a defence against Epigyne's demands, both sexual and social:

> You can help. Do up the house. Turn to in the garden. Talk to me, make me laugh, take me out, pamper me, show some affection, be my *man*! I'd rather have third shares in some other woman's virile husband than exclusive rights on a milksop.

His withdrawal is strategic since he wishes to avoid suicide, knowing that 'the price of love is death'. The awareness is with him always and his wife does nothing to ease his intimation of mortality:

[1] See, for instance, *Francis Bacon* by Rothenstein and Alley, 1964, number 152 'Lying Figure' 1959; number 154 'Lying Figure' 1959; etc.

> GONAD: Let me kiss your open grave.
> EPIGYNE: Your end is near.

As ever in Mr Warner's theatre sex, war and death are inextricably mixed. Their marriage is a 'germ-war of words" and Epigyne sees sexual politics as 'a moral equivalent of war'. Sex acts as a catalyst to release the violence and shortly after copulation Gonad is striking Epigyne. After learning that Guppy has sex 'just to kill time', sexual violence finds its apotheosis in the castration of Xyster, the lancing of the boil of poisonous delight. Xyster pays for destroying the cosy triangle by being changed into two sides of meat. Before this the curtains are drawn back to reveal the mirror cyclorama of Act II. How many images do the audience see in the cyclorama?

> Each man has two women, each woman two men. All eight of us poisoned by delight.

Epigyne expresses her awareness of the dual rôle they have each been performing. But Xyster's rôles are not those anticipated. She has been mistress to both men and wife to neither. Having created the lie as they all have, unlike the others she fails to go on living with it. If they have two rôles presumably they are both reflected in the mirror. We are thus confronted with sixteen images. In this continually proliferating maze what hope is there of locating a substantial human being?

> The invisible, the moments of happiness, are more real, however dreamlike, than the visible world of time.

The mirror shows us not only a reflection but an inverted picture. In the mirror everything is back to front as Guppy shows in Act II, describing Epigyne's appearance for the benefit of the audience:

> You're a bundle of contradictions! Your back tells me your front is false, and your false front confirms that your back is telling the truth. If it's wrong, it's right, and if it's right, it's wrong.

The mirror is the instrument of paradox and is therefore assured a crucial position in Warner-land. While the Groom of *Emblems* studies his 'Daily Mirror', we hear the wedding march back-to-front.

The mirror also acts as an alienation device for the audience, or at least for that part of it which can see itself in the mirror. In the words of Sapphira, the audience become voyeurs along with the actors 'watching themselves watch themselves create'. They are thus reminded that they are sitting in a theatre, a place created by an artist. They are in fact in a version of Hesse's hall of mirrors, constructed for the liberation of the imagination to bridge the gulf which life usually throws up between the imagination and external reality. The proliferation of images in a limited space reduces the probability of the spectator picking out the substance from the shadow and he is thus initiated into the same area of uncertainty that the actors inhabit. The Elizabethan slang term for an actor was a 'shadow', as in Puck's epilogue to *A Midsummer Night's Dream*: 'If we shadows have offended'. In other words the actor bears the same resemblance to the rôle he plays as the shadow does to the substance. But though the part may be more substantial than the actor, the rôle cannot come into being except through the medium of that actor. It is a paradoxical dependence fully exploited by a theatre such as Mr Warner presents, not bound by the contingencies of plot.

Consider the final scene of *Killing Time*. It seems to be building to a climax of violence with the torture of Chalone—a moment comparable with the castrations of Xyster and Ensoff. But we should have picked up the earlier clue. The guillotining of Quark was only a mock execution; the torture of Chalone is a charade played out to enable Phagocyte to divulge what he knows. Violence, as has been noted before, releases lyrical intensity of feelings which seem to lie at a deeper level than conventional rôle-play can expose. The extra stress imposed by the proximity of a violent act provides the incentive to talk. In *Killing Time* the utterance is predominantly in prose, but none the less the quality of Phagocyte's reminiscences is very different from his earlier more cryptic style. That Chalone was pretending is no reason to believe he was not suffering. The extent of his suffering depends on the depth of his emotional involvement in the part:

Pretending is extraordinarily exhausting. It's terribly hard work.

The difference lies in the speed with which he can detach himself from the pretence. From the shooting of Phagocyte to the end of the play we watch the actors of the parts of Squaloid and Chalone increasingly alienating themselves from their rôles. We learn more about the actors and less about their parts, a knowledge which takes us farther away from the situation of the play and gives us a clearer idea of what it is we think we have seen. The process is complete when the lights go down for the last time:

> The parts of actors are like flames of matches, blown out in the wind, and vanished.

In the theatre, however, pretence is as real as actuality. The torture of Chalone is therefore no more or less of a pretence than the shooting of Phagocyte. Rôles have been played as we saw them played in *Lumen*.

War has its own rules, more rigid and hierarchic than the peacetime world. We learnt from Chalone in his rôle as executioner, the most effective stopping agent of all, that 'war is a fever in our brain' and since the imagination is not confined in the limits of time this war is not set in any particular period or place though its language and references make it unmistakeably twentieth century, an amalgam of all previous war experiences. Squaloid, the universal soldier, has seen it all:

> It's my third war. Great War, Second War, and now this.

His recollections have the same tone as the Old Man's grim account in *Troat*, but unlike the Old Man he is still actively engaged in hostilities. He knows the real enemy is within:

> It's not war you should fear. It's fear.

Unlike the other plays, the soldiers are not married. War has replaced marriage as the theatre in which the characters 'with joy, tenderness and delight . . . transform themselves into beasts'. Once the transformation is complete they will be powerless to prevent the suicide of a world. There is no shortage of evidence in the plays of this degradation but it is not quite the entire picture, not even in *Killing Time*. The paradox of suicide may be that it gives to man the power of life and death over his destiny:

But you can argue that this ability of man also implies its opposite, and that—may—save us from the holocaust.

As with the other characters who embody wisdom, there is considerable discrepancy between what they do and what they say. In his actions we see that Chalone treats human beings as mere players of rôles, pieces in his chess game, where movements are controlled and predictable, but his words run deeper:

> The peace of this world is no more than the peace in each one of us; in you, in me: the love that refuses to hate. It's the withdrawal of imagination we must study; in marriage, in torture, or a mercenary.

In his summary of the theme of *Requiem* he seems to speak for the playwright. But is this the actor speaking or do the 'borrowed robes' of priesthood carry these sentiments sewn in their lining?

The juxtaposition of birth and death continues as fiercely as in *Lying Figures*:

> In India once I saw a woman burying her children one after another like an open womb.

The image is an echo of Vladimir's soliloquy at the climax of *Waiting for Godot*:

> Astride of a grave and a difficult birth. Down in the hole, lingeringly, the grave-digger puts on the forceps.

The paradox of death in life haunts the imagination of both Mr Beckett and Mr Warner, who sees the grave as the mirror image of the womb. It is also the connecting trap-door between life and death. It is the patch of sky in which the prisoners of death can notice the changes in life:

LAZ: From the perspective of death, life looks a little grave.

Since there's a war on, whores have taken the place of wives. Too long spent in an all-male situation such as the army causes the soldiers to adopt a boarding-school attitude to women, so that for the first encounter between the sexes we see the women dressed like whores but walking on stilts. It is the same attitude which dominates Harold Pinter's *The Homecoming* where the woman is simultaneously addressed as a prostitute and revered as a mother.

The mentality of the soldiers finds its counterpart in the lesbian relationship between Kuru and Quark:

KURU: Even if we have fallen in love, let's remain good
        friends.
QUARK: I hid from you when you arrived as I was afraid of
        myself.

The relationship demands masculine characteristics from one of the partners and can therefore be seen as a manoeuvre in the game of dominance, as is clear from the coupling of Bride One and Bride Two in *Emblems*.

The pattern of relationships in *Killing Time* is more confusing than in the other plays. Much of the dominant-subservient theme handled elsewhere by the females occurs here in the relationship between Squaloid and Phagocyte who becomes Squaloid's victim; the old soldier initiating the younger one into the ways of war as Wrasse initiates Callisterne into the ways of sex, then eliminating him when he fails to come down to scratch. The relationship between Kuru and Quark appears to be of the same order, but ultimately whores are just commodities of war, ammunition for the soldiers. Before that time Kuru displays some of the characteristics of Epigyne and Wrasse, particularly when preparing Quark for her mock-execution, but reveals her compassion as Ensoff does when comforting Callisterne:

> Close, close tight buds, now parting ends the day
>   Laughter must cease
> Colours fade, and withering winter come.

Her post-violence lyricism echoes strongly Sapphira's aubade at a similar moment in *Lying Figures*:

> Yet say, even as you droop
> And nod down to the roots from which you grow,
>   The shadows know
> Even as they stretch their fingers on the lawn
> No parting's loss when lovers long for dawn.

When beauty gives way to wisdom in the second stanza of her poem, her relationship to the action of the play is comparable to Agappy's as the source of spiritual love in *Meeting Ends*. As frequently happens in Shakespearian theatre the words of the

playwright speak through the character, who has already been
shown to be capable of taking on any rôle:

> Seal up, sweet lids, the trembling of damp eyes
>   And glistening cheeks;
> Strength is a beauty only known in grief:
>   Like men at war
> Who find true comradeship in cruelty,
>   And bravery
> Even as they mourn the very friends they kill—
> So may this night of parting bind us still.

Nevertheless there is perhaps too great a profusion of rôles for
one actress adequately to hold together or for an audience to
grasp at one viewing. The greater pace of *Killing Time* frequently
gives rise to difficulties of comprehension, but such problems do
nothing to cloud the intense beauty and joy of the moment.
Quark's gratitude at being handed back her life overflows into
spontaneous song and dance, a hymn to the force of human love,
which provides an antidote to Chalone's vision of the future
outlined at the start of the play.

The paradox of life in death is highlighted by Kuru's
acquiescence to the sexual urge during the funeral service, and
the links between sex and violence are made explicit by her in
her conversation with Quark in the verbose garden scene.
Though it aids comprehension, the scene deals in abstract form
with concepts made concrete in other scenes. It is justifiable
philosophically but not entirely theatrically. However, Mr
Warner's ability to summon up the telling image suddenly lifts
the conclusion of the scene on to a higher level:

QUARK: The trees are full of tears. There are flames! It's
dark. What's happening? The stars are too frightened
of these flowers of light.
KURU: The stars give out light, that's why you can see
them; but the black hole of war sucks in everything,
even light itself.

War is once again allied with sex and life flickers like a candle
in the night. Darkness is everywhere, for they are all involved in
war's night manoeuvres. The bees, whose queen—like Epigyne
—kills those it mates with, change their nature at night and

become dangerous. The time to catch eels, the symbol of the penis, is at night. The battle between light and dark wages incessantly throughout the *Requiem*. Though the light is always in danger it is not finally extinguished. The paradox is embodied in the frail figure of the blind Quark:

> My birthday's February 2nd, Candlemas. Snowdrops are emblems of the Feast of Lights!

However, the humans who are only distinguished by the vices of their night activities are afraid when trapped in the beams of the 'dazzling eyes of God':

> Emptiness enfolds. Darkness encroaches on the light, and in lightness we dare not comprehend.

With the words of the funeral service ('ashes to ashes, dust to dust') echoing behind the plays, Chalone's final words take us back to the opening of *Lying Figures* where Gonad tips ash into the corpse's mouth:

> Pray for those whose mouths last week were stopped by human violence, with dust.

Killing Time, though the second in the trilogy, was the last to be written, the playwright completing a circle which is never broken for in the beginning is its end.

The circle is the dominant shape of *Meeting Ends*, as the rectangle of the grave was of *Lying Figures* and the square of the chess board of *Killing Time*. The spirit of contradiction continues unabated as the Last Post sets the action off back to front while reminding us that we have reached the last post on the *Requiem* trail. The killing time of war is over and evening draws on apace. The sunshaft evoked by Ensoff is only one ray of light in the gathering gloom, a tiny flare of reason in the voodoo night of sensuality. Ensoff stands apart from the action, literally in a sphere of his own. Like the three wise men, paradoxically from the west, he looks from the Moon, the controlling planet of the trilogy, down to the Earth; the opposite perspective from Laz and Sapphira looking up from the grave:

> . . . And yet Earth looks so small, so blue,
> So lovely an oasis, that a spark
> Of heaven might once have touched some one-celled life:

> But mastodon, or grain of wheat, or shark—
> Gross fantasy; and for man to be true?
> Reason rejects such lunacy run rife.

Will a closer inspection of the planet continue to reveal such beauty? Ensoff has to summon up the courage to face the monster he has himself called into being. The structure of *Meeting Ends* is the most satisfying because Ensoff and Agappy are integrated into the action as Laz and Sapphira cannot be, and yet they maintain a detachment only occasionally achieved by Chalone and not at all by Kuru who is nominally Chalone's wife, though the relationship is only referred to in one scene.

The women aspire to different types of fulfilment, represented in the contrasting possibilities of the Jewish god, Ensoff and the voodoo god, Shango; light and dark. Agappy, like Sapphira, is past the age of sensuality and is already in the kingdom of Ensoff. The predatory Wrasse relates all experience to the sex war and belongs firmly in the world of Shango, while Callisterne suffers longings which are almost irreconcilable. Agappy is not thinking about cremation any more so she will become like Sapphira, a corpse, and she shares Sapphira's capacity to grasp the paradox of existence in the reversal of the expected order:

> Even in the best things, old men are childish till they're cradled in the grave.

Yet Sapphira appears before Agappy in the trilogy, illustrating further that in *Requiem* there is only one continuous moment containing all that has been and all that is to come.

Callisterne works at night like the Old Man and Gonad, but in her case the moon will be up so that Ensoff can watch over her. At her auto-erotic climax when the power of Shango is most dangerous, Ensoff is close by and is being drawn back to Earth where he must confront Shango:

> Yet should I think
> That there was no mistake—this was for me?
> Within whose skull old wary spiders prey
> And for whose throat a grey bird whets its beak?
> Sure, it can't be
> Unless the world's grown young and lost dismay
> And tears can laugh, and softest touch will stay.

Since we learn that the telephone is the only true darkness, it is the appropriate medium through which Shango can operate. Linked to the Groom by his newspaper and to Squaloid by his preference for absent love, we see him supreme where he can choose his weapons. But what we see and he does not is the mousetrap, and sure enough the trap is sprung. As with Kuru and Quark in the bath-chair scene, so here with Shango and Wrasse, the dominant-subservient treadmill turns a semicircle and Shango suffers for his past complacency. He is now trapped in Fortune's wheel which is also the cage in which he must sing for his supper. He will not find relief until the light starts to fall and the wheel casts its shadow in the shape of the sun-dial. With the aid of the darkness in the atmosphere of the jungle he will claim Wrasse back. Her dominance, like Bride Two's, is asserted in her change of costume. She is now the ring-master in a circus where Shango is the main attraction. As master of the ring she is of course the controlling figure in the marriage, and since Shango is in the ring she therefore has him wrapped round her finger. The vicious circle of matrimony of which the ring is the symbol is complete and he is left to his lonely suffering.

The grim legacy of Mr Warner's migraine is turned to brilliant artistic account in Shango's monologue of defiance which finds its counterpart in Agappy's monologue of acquiescence. His final defeat before the power of Ensoff is foreshadowed in his acknowledgement of divinity whose presence, as in other plays, is closely linked with physical suffering: 'If there is a God he lies in the teeth of pain'. At least some of the ambiguity of 'lies' is dispelled in the effect of this pain:

At least pain asserts the power of human pity, if only for oneself.

Life reaches a crisis point when the flesh starts to crumble. If the moment can be conquered, calmer waters are beyond. Bride Two recognizes the critical phase:

Thirty's a terrible age and thirty-five suicidal.

Agappy, with the help of the Highway Code, has seen herself through and earned the space to look back if not with wisdom at least with what Laz elsewhere calls 'an awareness of our unwiseness':

It's illegal for a horse to die at thirty-five. And if it's true for horses...

Her reminiscences call to mind the machinations of Wrasse and Shango:

I made a man's love the centre of my life. My own selfish passion of universal importance! When it failed, chaos came.

But more recent experience summons almost the same image that Chalone used at the conclusion of *Killing Time*, and the echo reminds us that we are listening to an actress, a living person, as well as an immortal character, for the experience evoked is universal as Mr Warner's prose reaches its highest point in the trilogy:

I was walking in black down a rainy street like a burnt match thinking how nettles grow and breed. 'Be charitable', he said. Well, I thought, chastity stirs the passion it's supposed to restrain! But an act of faith is an act of love. The gate badly needed some more creosote. Plants and grasses push up with the force of whirlwinds. There was blood. Evanescence in a stain. Be gentle with weakness. I too have shared dinner in Eden. Let's leave it vague. At best we are worthless, and at worst a little experienced. There's dew on the grass-blade and a creeping mist.

With the coming of old age passion is transformed into compassion.

The climax of the play is again a juxtaposition of violence and lyricism, and the most powerful yet for the victim of the violence is also the speaker of the lyric. Ensoff's castration is the counterpart of Xyster's in *Lying Figures* and between the two comes the anal insertion of *Killing Time*, an act of violence common to both sexes.

Ensoff's rejection of the bull's head indicates that he has not submitted himself to the power of Shango whose gesture is denied point since it lifts Ensoff above passion rather than reducing him below it. Like Oedipus he needs a stick for support and, also like Oedipus, through maiming his understanding has been enriched. He stands at the very centre of the sun-dial and at the centre of the circle formed by the ring of candles. He is at the still point of the turning world, protected by the circle or halo of light. Candles are a potent image in Mr Warner's theatre. Besides being a means of measuring the passing of time or, in their modern equivalent the flashbulb, stopping time to keep the past in the present as at the start of *Emblems*, the candles are also the source of life, a phallic symbol:

> SAPPH: Have you a candle for me, for when my fridge is off?
> LAZ: In your vanity bag.

Yet candles are also lit to commemorate the dead and both functions are suggested at the conclusion of *Lumen*. All the plays end with a pin-point of light in the thickening darkness, a hope for individual life amid the social gloom. Light and dark is a paradox extending to the Earth itself which must always be half in light, half in darkness. The light and the dark must both be accepted before integration can be attained:

> To understand the uninterpreted
> Half of this (*indicating audience*) mighty globe, till it reveals
> What teeming recompense can keep man warm.

As in the world, so in the theatre; the stage is lit while the audience is dark and when the lights go down on the stage they come up in the auditorium. The stage action is only half the image. It is the mirror held up to the audience.

At the conclusion of *Meeting Ends* this image is brighter, for the candles still burn and their shape symbolizes eternity. The words, too, support the image:

> Yet at my feet a snowdrop breaks moon's winter
> Its secret yellow trussed up in green gauze
> Traced round and rimmed with white, and all enfolded
> By three white lips that shield it out of doors,
> Weighing down like a bell from a sheathed splinter
> This surge of life the icy dust has moulded.

Killing Time ended on the word 'dust', but *Meeting Ends* suggests the first tiny step towards regeneration. The snowdrop is the first flower that breaks winter's grip, like a candle flaming in the dark. We need not doubt that we are hearing the playwright's authentic voice, for in the plays of Mr Warner the change from prose to verse is a guarantee of truth just as in the Shakespearian theatre it is an indication of nobility. At the moments of great emotional intensity like the birth of Gonad's child, the lyric subconscious bursts to the surface.

Ensoff, like Prospero, is hurt by his renewed contact with the world of men, but, as with Prospero, the experience does not quite cause him to lose his compassion; rather it gives it an opportunity to flower. At the moment when he has least cause for trust he expresses the power of human love in images which form the climax of the trilogy:

> The notes lie stilled as dusk folds down the fields.
> Sleep, my sweet lady, here, where all art lies;
> Summer's enchantment all its glory yields
> And airy wonder fills your closing eyes.
>
> Rest, while the masters of our waking joys
> Rule over us and stretch the oceans' clutch:
> The silent stars play havoc with our toys
> But we have kingdoms that they cannot touch.
>
> Lighten your dreams beyond the reach of thought,
> Skill's farthest limits are within these arms;
> And in the circle that our warmth has bought
> Your safety's milk lies soft between my palms.

The havoc has come and gone and the stars have all been shot, but the candles burn on. This is a requiem for the living and can never stop. So the bugle summons us back to the awakening of *Maquettes* and, like Finnegan, we too must begin again.

10

Suheil Bushrui

The Poetry

I

Although Mr Warner is a playwright with a widespread and growing reputation, and I have every respect for his dramatic ability, it is upon his poetry that I would like to concentrate, for it is in this field that perhaps one finds him using his linguistic skills to their capacity. Of these not the least evident is Mr Warner's versatility, his ability to compose an allegory in the true spirit and tradition of Spenser, or sonnets that embody the refractory complexities of modern consciousness. Mr Warner's language, like his technique, is an instrument of many uses. Its rhythms can mimic a newt, its clarity picture nature at its most vivid and beguiling, in a stream or a mountain prospect, and he can also use its syntax and vocabulary to tackle the intellectual processes, the lucubrations of the modern mind. Whether he uses language like a delicate brush, or a weapon to wrest from meaning its most difficult truths, Mr Warner's skill is manifest.

Such are his multifarious talents that perhaps the best approach to the poetry of Francis Warner is one that shows various facets of his work. This essay, therefore, seeks to examine, in the kind of detail they deserve, some of the poems that, to my mind, most evince his versatility, and which ultimately disclose to analysis a perfect synthesis, the unified individuality of his poetic voice.

II

One of Warner's most powerful poems, which confronts the greatest mystery of life—death—is undoubtedly *Plainsong*. Two of the author's young pupils committed suicide within months of each other, and *Plainsong* is inscribed 'In memory of Angus and David', with the epigraph 'Reapt ere half ripe, finisht ere half begunne', taken from Thomas Edward's famous couplet about Sir Philip Sidney:

And thou Arcadian knight, earthes second Sunne
Reapt ere half ripe, finisht ere half begunne.

To understand the significance to Warner of this personal
tragedy, it is essential to see it in the light of his religious beliefs.
In another poem, *For A Child*, combining neo-Platonism with a
Blakean verse technique (inspired, no doubt, by the study of
Blake made by Warner's close friend, Kathleen Raine[1]), Warner
converses with a squirrel who convinces him that:

> 'You are sleeping in this life
> In a shadow world of strife;
> Yet when the dream grows old and lame
> You will wake to life again.'

That Warner should express this philosophy through the simple
squirrel is characteristic of his view of faith. In an early poem,
The Love of God, he writes:

> No priest, with sanctuary bell,
> No rhetoric of demagogue,
> No missionary infidel
> Brings me to the love of God.
>
> But simpler state of mind,
> Seeing less, perceives the truth:
> A milkboy, whistling down the wind
> Theologically uncouth—

Warner's faith is deliberately unsophisticated and inspired by
what is most natural and immediate to the senses. So it is that
the death of his pupils moves him deeply, and obliges him, not
to rely on an inherited and received reaction, but to face the
issue personally and therefore forcefully; to absorb in his own
being the full shock to which, as a sensitive man, his senses are
open and vulnerable.

> . . . Two warm and living friends
> Wasting in mud and loam: suddenly snuffed
> On reaching manhood. One, and now another.
> Why, why oh why is this bitterness of doubt,

[1] See her acknowledgement to him: Kathleen Raine, *Blake and Tradition*
(2 vols), Princeton University Press [Bollingen Series XXXV, 11], 1968,
p. x. (Written 1964.)

> This thud of guilt and loneliness of despair,
> Impossible, titanic weight of a universe
> Balanced to try each one of us in turn?

Warner holds strong moral views and believes the poet has an important rôle to play in society. He has expressed these convictions in an essay entitled 'The Poetic Imagination':[2]

> ... the preference for taking the poet as the moral centre of the nation's health springs from a belief that, whereas the others are intermittently concerned with moral choices, the poet continually is.
>
> To an extent even greater than the theologian, let alone the priest, he is concerned with choices in that his entire professional life is concerned with the central question of relevant juxtapositions.

Warner sees clearly, therefore, that the poet is involved with morality not only as a man, a responsible individual, but by the very nature of his art. The poet's language is itself at the centre of his morality. So it is that in *Plainsong* Warner seeks the solution to the problem of death in the heart of language. So it is that he strips from his language the tried and easy literary responses to the brutal facts:

> I must not pose, colour or decorate
> And clothe an ugly fact: lament Adonis,
> Or mourn on Lycidas's golden urn.

Thus Warner penetrates the superficial and faces with his pen 'the brute impact of shattering moment on soul'. He knows that it is his duty as a poet to:

> ... bend the verse
> And wrest from it an iron ore of truth
> Stripped of accretions made from imitations:
> Lift up that flap of the brain and journey in
> To grip the bit and bridle of the heart.

Warner's desperate and heartfelt grief is explicit in his imagery. He sees the heart vividly as a runaway horse, wild with remorse, and he must penetrate beneath the intellect, through 'that flap

[2] Western Mail Literary Review, March 5, 1966, p. 9.

of the brain', to master the heart, 'to grip [its] bit and bridle'. He must penetrate beneath the intellect because 'meanings have no meaning when intellect battens on raw emotion'. The man faced with deep sorrow who relies on argument or logic is 'a whistling ant on an orange', a metaphor that aptly expresses the impotence of human rhetoric. The poet repudiates the facile answers, 'wild posturings, word-spun distractions', and determines:

> To realize each moment as it comes,
> Naked, for what it is . . .

He must face the plain, bare world, uncoloured by emotion and poetic sentiment: 'A dust-filled crack between two flooring boards', a tree 'stripped to its branches while the wind blows cold'.

Determined to take action 'to force corroding images away, lest grief becomes a luxury', the poet ventures out at night into a winter storm which exteriorizes, like the storm in *King Lear*, the turmoil of the inner thoughts, while the bleak winter landscape reflects the death, in sympathy, of nature and the shadows of the night match his own dark gloom.

Distracted by grief the poet walks on and on, coming to city streets only to reject them as a 'landscape of suffering worse than my own'; to feel, like Cowper, that 'God made the country and man made the town' and that the city offers only 'man-made mortality'. So the poet's journey continues to a lonely inn 'to find pure solitude', as he tries to come to terms with his grief. Only there, he believes, can he 'cool this cook and windmill of a mind'. He sees the turmoil of his thoughts as if they were a cook brewing within him or a windmill churning and boiling: wild images that display graphically the poet's desperate striving through metaphor to illuminate the nature of the terrible experience he is reliving by means of his night journey.

The poet highlights this tragedy of his emotions by contrasting the natural life of summertime 'when silver willows grew' and a 'sleeping snail . . . sunbathed on a log' with the present scenes of desolation:

> Unsheltered coltsfoot shiver on the bank,
> And bindweed claws and chokes the fishy reeds.

Once again the inner emotions are objectified in nature as the poet finds in wildlife, replete with lugubrious detail, the sympathy with his state of mind that he seeks. Warner's language as well as his imagery harmonizes with his feelings. The soft sibilants of the 'sleeping snail' are counterpointed with the hard alliterative 'c's of 'claws and chokes' so that the sound reinforces the sense.

At this point in the poem Warner breaks from the pentameter suited to the dramatic narrative and writes quatrains of Ballad metre (alternate and rhyming tetrameter and trimeter) and the reader is immediately and appropriately reminded of *The Rime of the Ancient Mariner*.

> The lonely fens are dark tonight
>   And swept by wind and rain.
> The watcher in the lonely house
>   Deaf to the windowpane.
>
> A wanderer with a hurricane lamp
>   Moves by the river side.
> A mother mourns in the candlelight
>   Silent and glassy-eyed.

The poet has projected himself into another wanderer, as Coleridge did with the Mariner, and he visits a mother mourning for her son and sits in vigil in the lonely, death-stricken house, deep in the desolate fens.

The poem continues after this interlude and as dawn breaks the poet has a monstrous vision of an apocalypse:

> What is that speck in the north? That growing cloud
> Approaching, blackening the air? The midnight bull
> Mighty, primaeval, bursting from the sky
> To butt this worthless bubble globe aside
> Trampling the fair and circus of mankind
> Like clover in a field: thirsting for death
> His horns rip up the heavens and cyclones swoop
> Wresting up trees and rocks, swamping the land
> Beneath a sheet of sea.

The terrifying spectacle of the holocaust purges the poet and enables him to measure the proportion of his human grief against the elemental chaos of nature. The cycle of human life is seen as part only of a greater whole: the cycle of the elements in Empedoclean terms. The 'waters that cover the earth promise a new healing refreshment', a binding together by Love of what has been separated by Strife, as the continual flux of the elements reorders the world. As Empedocles wrote: 'Of all mortal things there is no creation nor destruction by baneful death; only a mingling and a separation. Creation and death are but names given by men.'[3]

III

Perennia is an extraordinarily accomplished poem for a young poet of 23, and it is extraordinary too, in its conception, for a poem written in the 1960s. It was composed in a mere three weeks in the library of St. Catharine's College, Cambridge, before that library had been redesigned and where, during the summer vacation, the poet had the place to himself and, in his own words, 'time stood still'. *Perennia* has been through three editions and, somewhat to the author's amusement, it is one of his most popular works. It is not hard to see why.

The epigraph at the beginning of *Perennia*, from Edgar Wind's classic study, *Pagan Mysteries in the Renaissance*, is taken from a passage in a chapter on a medal of Pico della Mirandola's, where Wind is elucidating the philosophy of the Renaissance neo-Platonist, Marsilio Ficino:

> Only by looking towards the Beyond as the true goal of ecstasy can man become balanced in the present. Balance depends upon ecstasy.

It is important, in order to understand the allegory of *Perennia*, to grasp the significance of this quotation and to examine its context, both in the philosophy of Ficino and in the poetry of Edmund Spenser. Indeed, any consideration of *Perennia* is doomed to superficiality unless it takes fully into account the deep importance for Warner of his study of neo-Platonism and of its traditions in English poetry.

The two main characters in *Perennia* are Eros and Perennia and in the tradition of allegory these are 'visibilia' which express, in personified form, Ecstasy and the Beyond, while their

[3] 'On Nature', Fragment 8.

relationship represents the paradoxical union upon which Balance depends. In *The Shepheards Calender*, Spenser expressed a similar union of Balance and Transcendence, for he, like Warner, had studied the neo-Platonists and Ficino in particular. For Spenser the union was exemplified by his juxtaposition of the apparently irreconcilable mottoes: 'in medio virtus—in summo felicitas'.

Now it is significant that Ficino began his philosophical career as an Epicurean. This makes his original Florentine Platonism so much the more sympathetic. For, although he burned his early Epicurean essays, Ficino retained a belief in worldly pleasure which tempered his Platonism and which even importantly developed his thought, and resolved in his mature philosophy the paradox which Warner quotes.

Warner's own views, I feel, are very close to those of Ficino, and through Warner's allegory there runs a thread of warmth and humanity through which is interwoven the sterner neo-Platonism. Warner loves the imperfect forms of this world not merely because they are the shadows of other and more perfect forms, and he lights them with his affection so that they shine with a worldly beauty of their own. They are more than mere Platonic figures (εἴδη) or Pythagorean pebbles (ψῆφοι); more than mere counters from which pure geometrical forms are made. For Warner the fateful doctrine of two worlds, the world of sense and the world of thought, is not absolute and 'the number' and 'the unlimited' (τὸ ἄπειρον) are not irreconcilable. Indeed their unity is a major theme of *Perennia*. This is allegory, not symbolism, to use the distinction made so clearly by C. S. Lewis.[4]

Like the best Platonism, derived from Plotinus, Warner's views are pre-Plato and Pythagorean. Warner says that 'he has read the whole of Kirk and Raven's *The Presocratic Philosophers*' and used that book considerably in *Perennia*, and certainly the use of the four elements of earth, fire, air and water in the poem reminds one immediately of Empedocles, that wayward disciple of Pythagoreanism who has been so misunderstood by those unable to comprehend in modern terms the very classical unity of his scientific and mystical writings. But Warner has not allowed his reading to show or his scholarship

[4] See *The Allegory of Love*, p. 45.

to obtrude and mar the beautiful simplicity of his poem with complex or overly esoteric reference.

As the meaning behind *Perennia* is neo-Platonist in inspiration so too is its matter. Apuleius' version, in *The Golden Ass*, of the love of Cupid and Psyche was influenced by his own devotion to the philosophy of Plato, and by his reading of the *Phaedo* and the *Republic* in particular. And it is his story which Warner has used as the basis for the narrative of *Perennia*.

The story of Cupid and Psyche was not invented by Apuleius. It is a folk-tale common to many cultures and is even said to be still current in countries as different as Scotland and India. Apuleius made the story his own by turning it skilfully into a Platonic allegory of the progress of the rational soul towards intellectual love. (Here again we find the resolution of the seemingly incompatible.) Warner has changed the name of the heroine from Psyche to Perennia, changed the name of Cupid's mother from Venus to Hespera and transferred the name of Salacia, the mischievous goddess of the sea, to Perennia's sister; but otherwise the story is, superficially at least, the same as in Apuleius.

Venus (Hespera) is jealous and angered because the beauty of a mere moral, Psyche (Perennia), has led to the neglect of her own worship. She asks her son, Cupid, to take revenge on Psyche by making her fall helplessly in love with a wretched mortal. But Cupid falls in love with her himself and the couple live happily (although, because Cupid comes at night, Psyche cannot recognize him) until Psyche's sisters in their turn become jealous and inspire her to investigate her lover's identity. In treacherously inspecting Cupid's features with a torch, Psyche accidentally burns him and he flees in pain to his mother who, discovering his disobedience and more determined than ever in her hatred, gives Psyche impossible tasks to fulfil. Psyche is able to accomplish these tasks because of the affection felt for her by the birds and beasts who help her. Thus she thwarts Venus and even visits the Underworld unscathed until, on her return, she glances into a box containing divine beauty, which sends her into a deathlike sleep. From this she is woken by Cupid, who has returned to her, and thus the story ends happily.

So Warner has appropriately chosen for his story a famous tale, one that is itself perennial. The plot and the characters are borrowed from the folk-lore of Europe and from Apuleius' Platonic treatment of the story. But it is the changes that Warner has made to the tale that are remarkable and show that he, like Apuleius before him, has made it his own. For, in notable respects, Warner has transformed his inherited material.

In Apuleius' version the love affair of Cupid and Psyche is set in Cupid's splendid palace; in Warner's poem the romance takes place in the famous garden of the god of love, in a natural setting, and the lovers retire to a cave. In other words Warner has given the story a pastoral turn. He deliberately contrasts the life of town and country and the poem begins with the poet's flight from the 'Piccadilly sights' and 'throbbing nights' of city life to the sylvan countryside, an opposition that is underlined by the poet's reference to the 'Eros statue' of Piccadilly Circus, a poor substitute for the god. The narrator then takes on something of the character of a shepherd and introduces the story by playing on his flute.

The use of the Pastoral tradition in the story of Cupid and Psyche is an innovation that enables Warner to give credibility to the tale, which, although set in a classical Arcadia, takes place plausibly in contemporary England. The romance is in the tradition of Theocritus and Virgil, but Perennia drinks 'honey-mead, the [English] country beer'. If Pastoral lives for us at all at the present time—if it is to be indeed perennial—then it lives by its capacity to move out of its old haunts to inhabit the ordinary country landscapes of the modern world. In transferring the Pastoral, Warner is giving it renewed meaning, as did Virgil in moving its setting from Sicily to Arcadia.

In England the main influence of neo-Platonism has been literary rather than philosophical, and this influence has been a continuous one from the Elizabethans to the Romantics—and even in modern times on Yeats. In the early medieval West, knowledge of neo-Platonism was meagre compared with Arab knowledge, and the impact of neo-Platonism on Moslem theology was notable as early as the eleventh century through the scholar al-Ghazzali (1058–1111); but with the Renaissance, Europe rediscovered Plato, and Dante's *Divine Comedy* was greatly affected, as can be seen from the concluding vision of that poem. As the Renaissance spread to England, Ficino's commentary on the *Symposium* and Giordano Bruno's *Eroici Furori* became major sources of Elizabethan ideas on love. Thus neo-Platonism began its influence on English poetry, an influence that continued to inspire even poets like Coleridge and Shelley, to whom were available all Plato's own texts and who could read him in the original Greek.

One of the great English poets attracted by neo-Platonism was, as we have seen, Edmund Spenser. The Platonism of the *Timaeus* and the *Symposium* was so congenial to his imagination that it quite possibly confirmed him, and quite certainly encouraged him, in his allegorical habit of conception and expression.

Spenser is a poet to whom Warner is in many ways comparable. Like Spenser who 'excelled in all kinds', Warner writes, with equal ease and success, allegory, pastoral or sonnet. And Spenser had too, like Warner, a genuine love of the country so that his haycocks, briars and bullfinches spring not from the Sicily of Theocritus or Virgil's Arcadia, but, like Warner's flora and fauna, from the English countryside. It was Spenser's love of nature which enabled him to earn such a reputation as a pictorial poet and it was this same felicitous gift of enjoyment of nature that caused W. B. Yeats to call Spenser 'the poet of the delighted senses'. How appropriate this comparison is to Warner's *Perennia* can be seen from this passage:

> A newt disturbed a clump of meadow-sweet
> And peered through clusters of marsh-marigold
> To catch a caddis-fly. His web-like feet
> Darted round crowfoot stems to find a hold,
> Or paused among those loosestrife buds which fold
> The purple flowers close within their leaves
> To shield them from night vapours and the cold.
> She watched him jerk and scamper by degrees
> On to a full-lipped lily, where he seemed to freeze.

That is only one of the many stanzas in *Perennia* which follow, one after another, unfolding a succession of descriptions filled with sonorous and visual richness. The poetry is

> ... sprinckled with such sweet variety
> Of all that pleasant is to eare or eye.[5]

Warner's affinity with Spenser is emphasized by his excellent choice for *Perennia* of the famous 'Spenserian stanza', the form

[5] *The Faerie Queene*, VI. Proem. I.

Spenser himself created for *The Faerie Queene* and which has since been used successfully by such poets as Shelley and Tennyson. This is a stanza of nine lines rhyming ababbcbcc and linked to its successor by an alexandrine. It is perfectly adapted to the style and subject of *Perennia*, for it permits endless variations of internal and external grouping, and hence is ideally suited to the depiction of the multiple vignettes and dissolving views which follow each other with such great variety in the poem. Also, because of the stanza's notable faculty of linking itself to the stanzas preceding and succeeding, the narrative, essential to the allegorist, is not interrupted. The sustained melody of the rhythm and the harmony of the rhymes combine in various and unpredictable beauty and the form shows Warner's musical talent as well as his pictorial vision:

> The river idled in among the weeds,
> Eddying round each obstacle that came,
> And lulled the sycamore's slow falling seeds
> That fluttered down to make a teasing game
> For hungry minnows, searching for a grain
> Or water-fly. The clouds born in the stream
> Drank in the sunlight and threw back again
> Flashes of warmth from where cool trout and bream
> Slept while the liquid music murmured through their dream.

Liquid music murmuring through a dream. Such is *Perennia*; which is a reflection of Warner's sensuous apprehension of the natural world in all its multiplicity and also a voyage in the realm of ideas. Philosophically, formally and thematically the poem represents a unified harmony of mind and body that is itself 'perennial'; a harmony that typifies both poem and poet, for Warner's greatest talent is the balancing of sense and intellect, of tradition and innovation, to speak in the timeless voice of 'peerelesse poesie'. Truly, in balance there is ecstasy.

IV

Like W. H. Auden, another poet who was steeped in the English tradition, and a winner, before Warner, of the Messing International Award for 'distinguished contributions to the world of literature', Warner has turned his hand to forms of a very dif-

ferent kind, forms from another—and one might have thought
inimical—tradition. Like Auden, Warner has written a Blues
and a Calypso, and these, published among the poems selected
for inclusion in the prize-winning collection, are worth examin-
ing as evidence of Warner's technical virtuosity and his pro-
ficiency with so different an art. Or is it so different? As Kathleen
Raine says: 'It is almost forgotten that the term 'lyric poetry'
meant words for music. Francis Warner has the gift of writing
words fit for songs . . .'

Warner's *West Coast Blues* has almost no punctuation and
misses it not at all, for the natural rhythms of the singing voice
need no help from literary devices. The rhymes, in the tradition
of the blues, are simple, straightforward masculine rhymes
(mind/find; day/say) and the stanzas run fluently into each
other so that the whole song flows freely with the melody implicit
in the form. It is difficult to quote without spoiling this effect,
but the first three stanzas give at least an indication of the style,
and show the poetic flourishes with which Warner has adorned
the form he has adopted so easily and naturally.

> I've tried so many women since I left you,
> I've tried so many ways to ease my mind;
> I've left my bed to drift through San Diego,
> But everything I do I always find
>
> The cold hands of the clock drag oh so slowly
> Dead conversations stifle out the day
> And nobody's body answers like your body
> Nothing can light me up the way you say
>
> 'I love you' when you wake up in the morning
> A naked lily crumpled in a sheet
> 'I love you' when your lips hang moist and open—
> All I can think of in this rain-washed street

The first verse is admirably within the blues idiom, with its
colloquialisms ('ease my mind'), while in the second Warner
blends in the poetic image ('Dead conversations stifle out the
day'). In the third he likens his love to a 'naked lily crumpled
in a sheet' and with a flash of metaphoric intuition connects the
freshness of 'the rain-washed streets' with his lover's 'lips hanging
moist and open'.

Warner is commenting wryly on the two sides of America, and he calls his Calypso *East Coast Calypso* in contradistinction to his *West Coast Blues*. In a rhythm that leaps and bounces with the best, the 'Calypso' compares the apparent glamour and attractions of New York with its seamier reality. For instance:

> Kennedy Airport's bright and gay
> Pink floodlight fountains make it look like day
> Everybody's rich and kissing and plush
> But down on the waterfront—hush! hush! hush!

That Warner can write so well in these idioms should cause no surprise; for in so doing he is bringing up to date the very commendable aims expressed by Wordsworth in the Preface to the *Lyrical Ballads*: to keep 'the reader in the company of flesh and blood' and to refresh poetic diction by bringing his language 'nearer to the language of men'. Like the Romantics before him, Warner delights in pure simplicity, and his technique, nourished at its roots by tradition, has a growth that spreads and encompasses the popular folk-song of modern times, as Wordsworth in his own day had espoused the ballad. Warner's verse speaks, whether through the medium of Pastoral or Calypso, with the unmistakable voice of today.

V

Francis Warner has written a sequence of sonnets, a sequence in the true sense of the term, and in the tradition begun by Sidney, for the poems are linked by common themes and their effect is cumulative. These are called *Experimental Sonnets* and, as that name implies, they represent a blend of modernity and tradition. Indeed it is from this tension between traditional form and modern content that Warner generates the power which enables him to forge a new language. This language is that of a tough, intellectual process, the struggle, through words themselves, towards meaning. The experiment has been a brave undertaking and, for the most part, a triumphant success, with an exacting rhyming scheme and taut, compressed rhythms combining to give new and vigorous life to the sonnet's traditional properties of wit and skilful expression—so that form and language, old and new, are unified and mutually reinforced.

The tenth sonnet begins:

> Was that white shape that lurched out of the night
> To suffocate our windscreen, breathing on
> Into the perched and blinded loneliness
> An owl?

That first sentence is typical of Warner's frequent and stimulating use of the rhetorical question. Doubts as to the true nature of this night creature are deliberately and pertinently evoked by this provocative opening. The creature's contradictory and even menacing aspects are emphasized by its description as a 'white shape', and its awkward appearance, 'lurching out of the night'. The bird is imagined and depicted in all its threatening strangeness to the car's passengers, alienated from nature, and ensconced in their driving machine. The living creature 'suffocates' the lifeless windscreen and itself 'breathes on'. This is no ordinary owl and its sudden appearance no mere accident. This is the visitation of a nature spirit in the tradition of the albatross, and the bird magically transfers its own qualities to the night—of which it is the emblem. Hence the night is 'perched and blinded' as an owl—but as an owl might be in daytime. For this is no rational being but an embodiment of paradox, the symbolic bird of wisdom whose truth transcends logic and petty human rationality.

The sonnet continues:

> . . . No prate of peopled England here.
> The headlights catch the cautious rabbits' play
> And romp them roadsiding, to widow past,
> Unkiss the shroud and lift the latch of dark;

'No prate of peopled England here'. Indeed not; the prate and prattle of cosmopolitan life, the hubbub of cosy conversation, the security of city life, are stripped from man in this elemental situation where he confronts nature in all its unnerving mystery. Warner's language, too, reflects this rejection of the familiarity of civilized speech as he reaches into the unknown, coining new words to describe a new world that spurns the customary, the habitual labels. So he invents 'roadsiding', used alliteratively with 'romp', and then continues with a new verb, 'to widow'; for here is an extraordinary metaphor: the car and its passengers are like a widow whose husband, nature, is dead but can be revived. The shroud can be lifted and the repressed memories unlocked by the shock of intimate contact. As Coleridge wrote:

> And in our life alone does Nature live:
> Ours is her wedding garment, ours her shroud.[6]

The headlights continue:

> Probing the bosomed, catseyed mist ahead
> Half-formed and damp; thick, intermittent, gone.
> This far-past-midnight world of deerhorned trunks
> And unrepentant fields so utterly ours
> We tread the edge of promise with the dawn.

Here the quality of mist is both impressionistically painted and symbolically pointed. The mist is like a shroud covering 'bosomed', maternal nature, punctuated with the cat's-eyes which remind us of the weirdly natural origin of man's most artificial inventions. It represents the mystery of nature and its fleeting forms are parted and vanish to reveal the night land-scape to which the human creature rightfully belongs; a natural landscape part-plant, part-animal, of 'deerhorned trunks' which loom out of the sky, and part-human too, for the fields are 'unrepentant' and belong to man so 'utterly' that the dawn becomes the dawn of man's rediscovery of his lost affinity with nature:

> New senses register. Relive all these
> As moving emblems of our sympathies.

These are, then, the 'moving emblems' in more ways than one. They are alive in the dark landscape of the unconscious and they can be brought to light by the awakening of new senses, our emotions. The emblems of our true sympathies, they are sign-posts on the symbolic road to our rediscovery of ourselves—of, as Coleridge says, the nature that lives within us.

In the thirteenth sonnet of the sequence Warner contrasts the exhilarating experience of nature with the cold despair of man's civilized existence, where there is loneliness in the midst of over-population and emptiness at the core of the clutter of what has been called the 'bric-à-brac réalist', the overwhelming prolifera-

[6] 'Dejection: An Ode'.

tion of objects with which man surrounds himself and to which
he has delegated only the signs of his presence.

> A towel; suitcase; this a hotel room.
> Each object, élite, curiously numb:
> Clean, empty place of unreality,
> All singly neat.

Here Warner has transferred the numbness of the human subject
to the objects that return to him only the 'unreality' of his own
touch. These objects, when patted like a dog, return no evidence
of reassuring life, but are each like 'the icy moment at the heart
of pain', cut off from each other, 'singly neat', belonging to no
pattern, sharing no relations and partaking of no significance.
This sonnet represents, in contrast to the preceding one, the
alienation of man in his man-made world, the 'mad traffic
hurtling on' as his own productions have exiled him to fright-
ened solitude and he must 'cross-lock the door', retreat, 'stay
numb'. This is the insane existence of modern man: 'Is there a
reason behind human care?' Can the poet venture in this world
'and come back sane'? This is the nightmare landscape of
human rationally-ordered madness; this is 'the acreage of its
despair'.

The eighteenth sonnet presents something of a relief to such
inspissated gloom, and suggests a brave solution to the trials of
existence. Alluding in his imagery to music, painting and
drama, Warner indicates the rôle of the artist in the modern
world. The artist must find the hidden order in the chaos around
him, and to do so must transcend the ephemeral emotions of the
moment, the second-hand reactions, in order to confront reality:

> Not in heat's self-paralysis of hate,
> But with compassion's quiet certainty;
> And neither flinch, nor find across [his] course
> Memories of unmitigated remorse.

Each of Warner's sonnets ends thus, in a rhyming couplet
which is a self-contained, aphoristic conclusion to the fierce
process of thought that precedes. This rhyming couplet is in the
tradition of the English sonnet, and was the principal innova-
tion of Wyatt to the Petrarchan sonnet. In Warner's sonnets
these ending couplets come with the relief of finality, when

thought and form are synthesized and a new truth has been wrested from the world by the effort of linguistic adventure and discovery.

Sometimes in these sonnets (and elsewhere in his work) Warner uses an intricate system of internal rhyme and half-rhyme. Such a sonnet is the twentieth, in which a mother experiences the shattering effect of her young son's death. The reactions of the bereaved parents are sensitively portrayed: while the mother sits, the father, whose predicament Warner shows with great understanding,

> . . . cloisters up
> His thoughts, attempts to play the comforter,
> Awkwardly; climbs beneath the roof to search
> For papers that he knows may not be there:

Warner's psychological acumen is apparent in this description of the father who feels that, with the loss of his son, he has misplaced his rôle. He tries 'awkwardly' 'to play the comforter', and then engages in the 'displacement behaviour' of those in situations of stress, performing even a meaningless action rather than do nothing.

However, it is the subtle rhyme scheme that gives the sonnet the necessary tautness of form, without what Milton disparagingly called 'the jingling sound of like endings':

> As in her grief a mother cannot clean
> The fingermarks left on the windowpane,
> But finds relief in sitting for a while
> Where he with deft impatience on the floor
> Tugged off his shoes, still knotted, by the fire.

The key words (for example, 'grief' and 'relief') are given the emphasis of rhyme without the inappropriate patness or obvious intrusion of end-rhymes. Yet the end of the poem, summing up the preceding scene and drawing from it a conclusion that illuminates with intelligence the nature of human bereavement, intentionally uses the finality previously avoided:

> As such emotion dreads to be betrayed,
> So, in the silent grief, one part's afraid.

Warner is a master of many techniques, but none is the master of him. He chooses carefully as well as variously, and suits the form to the content. In fact that notoriously invidious distinction is one that he transcends. In the Introduction to his *Early Poems* Warner writes:

> Poetry when it comes, both deserves and needs the finest material language can give . . . the truest moments of poetry are realised only when form and content, language and inspiration, are so interrelated that such divisions become impossible; when a compound, not a mixture, has occurred.

The twenty-first sonnet takes up and develops the theme of the thirteenth. The meaningless violence of modern life is shown as filling the emotional void depicted in the earlier sonnet. In uncompromising language Warner images the brutality of existence, a man-made brutality inflicted by man upon himself. This Warner shows symbolically as man's own instruments inflict the peculiarly human tortures that only man is capable of perpetrating:

> . . . stuttering hate snarls down the blade
> As a pneumatic drill rapes the dead quay:

This necrophiliac drill which mimics human perversion shows Warner's language at its wildest, as does another image from this sonnet: '. . . a drawing-pin studs in the eye / Of mind'. In the final couplet Warner realizes, as a dramatist, and as did Shakespeare, the dreadful irony of 'man's tragedy' that makes us 'gambol in our agony'.

The following sonnet (the twenty-second) again returns to a previous motif. So closely interwoven are these sonnets, that as each in itself works out and resolves a truth, its conclusion becomes the starting-point for yet another departure in this continuing debate with modern meaning. From the rôle of the artist considered in sonnet eighteen, Warner turns now to the rôle of art. Again the imagery is from music, painting and drama. The beauty of art is transient and fleeting, Warner suggests, alluding to the famous words of Heraclitus with the simile 'as time runs over an apple in the stream'. Art is like a play with a cast of court ladies from the paintings of Watteau, listening as time passes irreversibly, to the artful and highly ritualized music of Purcell and Mozart. 'Bear with me', writes Warner, 'if I leave such scenes behind: / The dark offstage preoccupies my mind.'

'The dark offstage preoccupies [his] mind'. This line, perhaps one of the most significant of the many resonant lines in these sonnets, raises the central question of the value of art in the cruel chaos of modern society. And yet (and here Warner is at his most subtly paradoxical), life is art itself—for it is grasped fully only by the metaphor of drama: 'the dark offstage'.

Sonnet twenty-three is one of the most linguistically daring of Warner's experiments. Logic zig-zags through language as Warner struggles to penetrate the barrier which guards truth. Cratylism is pushed to its limits where the things concealed by words appear. But one has to conclude that this poem, although a brave attempt, is flawed. Warner's vocabulary exceeds his power of expression and ultimately truth is obscured, not revealed, by the piling of multiple metaphor upon abstraction: 'Abrasive anger at such impotence [of the 'Grey waste of intricacy's heritage'] / To help the frailer by diviner part / Engineers atrophy of maimed desire / And nails inevitable reconciled.' One must admire the eloquence but admit that here the limits of meaning are exceeded. Nevertheless the sonnet represents a bold endeavour and a considerable achievement; there are few poets who have ventured so far into the labyrinthine tunnels of language, who have struggled so hard to test the linguistic strength of meaning.

The last two sonnets in the sequence explore the major theme of human mortality. The futility of human experience and the frailty of human achievement are poignantly acknowledged:

> Not in heat's self-paralysis of hate,
> But with compassion's quiet certainty.

For Warner's conclusions are not those of immature and rebellious nihilism but the fruit of deep contemplation, the considered opinion of one who sees life not from the prejudiced perspective of youth but with the bird's-eye view of adulthood. From 'the breaking dawn, the cry upon the bed' to 'mandarin manhood', sonnet twenty-four catalogues the human process symbolized by the bizarre objects of man's affection, each one imbued with his own mortality, even the most significant ultimately equal to the most banal:

> Books, Bibles, bidets; halls, hills, cottages;
> Flow and ebb of bodily seasons' tides;

> Those motley macaronics day and night;
> Companions—all the panoply of rust.

Again Warner returns to the image which he knows as a dramatist to be the awful, the ironic truth:

> No intermission from this pantomime
> Till termination bring an end to time.

Sonnet twenty-five, the last and perhaps the most beautiful of all, is written with the limpid clarity of truth, attained by the mental struggle with human destiny which has preceded. The poet now considers in tranquillity the emotions he has experienced—in life as in his art. Love, like summer, must pass in the cycle of human life as in the cycle of nature's seasons. In an image pregnant with wistful sorrow, Warner regrets that love 'should like a toy / A child has wearied of be tossed away'. The pure simplicity conceals a metaphoric depth. Human passion, in its most profound expressions, love and literature, is fleeting and evanescent, leaving only its signs:

> ... can this paper be the last that you
> Will hold of mine, these words end passion's qualms?

If the objects of man's innermost emotions are resonant it is because at the core they are hollow, and as their sounds die away, so does man. In his passion and his art man finds himself reflected and, like Narcissus, he is trapped and must pine away before his ghostly image, until the pool of his imagination is dried and gone.

> Strange how the mutability of things
> Evaporates all man's imaginings.

* * *

It is hard to evaluate a living writer and doubly hard when his writings are so close to the frontiers of modern literature. Not until the passage of time and further progress of literary exploration will the new boundaries be drawn, maps charted and the roads clearly marked. But, even now, we can safely say that no one else has so stretched the sonnet form (with all the elasticity of eloquence that it demands) from its early Elizabethan beginnings to incorporate the language and thought of modern times. Warner has placed the awkward shapes of modern consciousness carefully and sensitively within the fragile and delicate sonnet; so carefully that both the form and the consciousness have been transformed, the sonnet expanded, the consciousness delimited, until a harmoniously proportioned unity has been achieved. The sequence is truly a triumphant blending of tradition and modernity.

Ingrid Melander

Experimental Sonnets: A Study of Rhyme

I

The Elizabethan sonneteers liked to group their elaborate compositions on courtly love into series of varying length. The predominant type of sonnet was the English (or Shakespearean) variant of the Italian prototype built on three decasyllabic quatrains, alternately rhymed, with a concluding couplet. Perfection of this medium was attained in Shakespeare's sonnets, which also mark an extension and transformation of theme towards a more varied treatment of the predicament of human life. The salutary play of wit and irony in these sonnets enlivens the rigid pattern of a convention which, in the hands of lesser poets, frequently became overwrought and monotonous. The English sonnet form gradually lost its attraction, and poets ceased to compose sequences. For about two centuries the Italian type was favoured, and regarded as the 'legitimate' form. In the 1830s, however, the sonnets of Shakespeare and other Elizabethan poets began to appear in current anthologies, and this revival of the Elizabethan mode had some influence on the early Victorian love sonnet. After 1850 the sonnet sequence again became popular as a vehicle for the expression of personal experiences, Mrs Browning's cycle 'Sonnets from the Portuguese' being the first outstanding example. In spite of differences in style and structure between the Elizabethan and the Victorian sequence, the total impression of the latter is usually one of emotional kinship with the Elizabethan conception of this poetic medium.

In recent years a very conscious attempt to assimilate and further develop the technique of the Elizabethan sequence has been made by Francis Warner, who in *Experimental Sonnets* (1965) offers no less than a modern sonnet sequence conceived on the Elizabethan model. Broadly speaking, there is a striking similarity of theme between Warner's cycle and those of his predecessors, but a closer study reveals that here the conventional sonnet themes are employed with an immediacy of expression and a personal involvement that goes far beyond the codified practice of the Elizabethan sonneteer. Moreover, a greater variety of themes and moods have been brought within the compass of the sonnet, which goes to prove that the possibilities of this much used medium have not yet been exhausted.

Judged as a whole, the twenty-five 'experimental' sonnets which make up Francis Warner's sequence fulfil the poet's ambition as expressed in an interview in October 1976. He then declared that it is not enough for a modern poet merely to keep and use the best of what earlier generations of poets have attained—he should also infuse new life into traditional form and thought. When speaking of his sonnet sequence, Warner pointed out that noticeable innovations could be perceived in the realms of emotion and in rhyme technique. Since rhyme has always been considered a significant structural feature of the sonnet, it would seem justifiable to examine how far the poet's deployment of rhyme is 'experimental'. It is therefore the aim of this study to describe and analyse in some detail the distribution and quality of rhyme in *Experimental Sonnets*. Such an undertaking certainly involves the risk of over-emphasizing the importance of a single metrical device, but since Francis Warner himself points to the rhyme technique as one of his main concerns in his experimentation with the sonnet form, that risk might well be worth taking. However, in order to avoid making rhyme appear too decisive a factor for the total poetic effect, I will examine one of the sonnets and try to relate the poet's use of rhyme to the development of theme and also touch on its possible impact on the expression of emotion (see below, Part II).

On page 32 in *Experimental Sonnets*, the following intriguing note can be read:

> Most of the sonnets in this sequence change the traditional form by bringing many of the rhyme-words in from the end of lines, usually to the centre.

This information provides an important key to the poet's distribution of rhymes. The manner of placing rhyme-words within the lines rather than at the end is not a new phenomenon. In *A Linguistic Guide to English Poetry* (1969) Geoffrey N. Leech comments on the opening lines of Coleridge's 'Kubla Khan' pointing out the subtle interplay between different types of rhyming. In the second and fourth lines there is, incidentally, what Leech calls an 'internal rhyme' between 'pleasure(-dome)' and 'measure(less)' (p. 93). Another example is to be found in Wilfred Owen's poem 'Exposure', which has ache/awake in the first and second lines of the first stanza. However, nobody seems to have practised this method so deliberately and with such consistency as does Francis Warner in his poetry. In fact, we can find it fully developed even in his first collection of poems, for instance in 'Plainsong' written in 1962, and his use of this inventive technique within the rigid structure of the sonnet form must certainly be regarded as a novelty. In the interview referred to above, the poet called his device 'centre-rhyme', and this term will be used in what follows. An alternative choice would have been 'internal rhyme' (in accordance with Leech's usage), but since this term usually refers to the rhyming of words *within* the line (or possibly the rhyming of a word in one line with another in the next line), I feel that 'centre-rhyme' will prove a more adequate label for Warner's innovative rhyme, which is a substitute for end-rhyme. Admittedly, 'centre-rhyme' does not describe the exact position of the rhyme-words but merely hints at an approximate place near the middle or even, as in a few cases, at the beginning of the line. It should be noted that end-rhyme is used occasionally in the quatrains for specific purposes and always in the concluding couplet.

As a rule, the position of rhyme in Warner's sonnets thus differs strikingly from the rhyme-scheme of the regular Shakespearean sonnet form, which is end-rhymed according to the following well-known pattern: ababcdcdefefgg. Three out of twenty-five sonnets in Francis Warner's cycle retain this pattern unchanged, Nos. I, III, and XXV. The remaining twenty-two have centre-rhyme in the quatrains, sometimes reinforced by end-rhyme, according to the following tentative classification (Arabic numerals are used to denote rhyme in centre-rhymed sonnets):

Type 1: 12123434565677. Here belong Nos. II, VI, VII, IX,

X, XIV, XVII, XVIII, XIX, XX, XXI, XXII, and XXIII = 13 sonnets.

Type 2: 12312345645677. Here belong Nos. IV, V, VIII, XII, XV, and XVI = 6 sonnets.

In No. XV the rhymes may also be linked according to the following rhyme-scheme: 12213443566577. If this pattern is preferred—and some readers will certainly do so, largely because of the end-rhyme of lines 6 and 7 (law/straw)—still another type of rhyme-scheme will have to be added to the four categories listed here. I have placed this sonnet under Type 2, mainly because this alternative was favoured by the poet.

Type 3: 12123434566577. Here belong Nos. XI and XIII = 2 sonnets.

Type 4: 12213434566577. Here belongs only No. XXIV = 1 sonnet.

The above table of rhyme-schemes may seem neat and straightforward at first sight, but Francis Warner's use of centre-rhyme is, in effect, a most complex affair. The poet's deliberate experimentation with rhyme has resulted in an enlargement of the traditional notion of what is meant by rhyming, and therefore a great variety of sound parallelism will be found in his sonnets. It seemed a plausible conjecture that the poet's fondness for inventing new rhyme patterns might have been inspired by Wilfred Owen's innovative rhyme techniques, and this was confirmed by the poet himself in the interview of October 1976. It should be pointed out, however, that pararhyme, which was used so admirably in Owen's mature poetry, does not occur in Warner's sonnets, but his frequent deployment of assonance and consonance produces rhyme effects which are similar in kind to those in Owen's poems, and which help to create unusually vivid and complicated sound patterns.

As a structural unit centre-rhyme does not differ from end-rhyme. It thus contains the same kinds of sound parallelism as does traditional end-rhyme, the most common type being rhyme proper or full rhyme. The customary division into mono-syllabic ('masculine') rhymes, disyllabic ('feminine') rhymes, and polysyllabic rhymes also applies to centre-rhyme. Not unexpectedly, full rhyme is the most frequent type, as in No. XX, where all the rhyme-words are 'masculine': grief/relief, left/deft, shoes/news, walk/talk, times/climbs, and play/may. 'Feminine' rhymes occur, for instance, in No. IX: certain/curtain (lines 1 and 3) and in No. XI: oceans/motions (lines 10 and 11); such word pairs as operation/preparation (lines 3 and 6 of No. V), benediction/dereliction (lines 2 and 4 of No. XI), and attitude/platitude (lines 10 and 11 of No. XV) may be quoted as examples of polysyllabic rhymes.

The rhyme-words listed so far look conventional enough, but *Experimental Sonnets* contains a large number of rhyme pairs which stand out as remarkable novelties, at least within the structure of the sonnet form. I am referring to instances of the following kind, which coincide more or less with Coleridge's rhyme of 'pleasure(-dome)' and 'measure(less)' mentioned above: (whip-)crack/back(bone) in No. VI (lines 9 and 11), whether/feather(breath) in No. XII (lines 2 and 5), and flesh/press(ure) in No. XV (lines 1 and 4). Even bolder inventions of centre-rhyme occur, where the rhyming elements do not form morphological units but consist of parts of words which in themselves convey little or no meaning. The following are such rhymes: (abso)lute/brut(alize) in No. VIII (lines 9 and 12), (cyni)cize/(ho)riz(on's) in No. VII (lines 5 and 7), and (prac)-tition(er)/(compo)sition in No. XVIII (lines 6 and 8). These rhymes reveal a close kinship to some of Hopkins's innovations, for instance the 'broken' rhyme of sing/ling-(ering) at the ends of lines 6 and 7 in the sonnet beginning 'No worst, there is none'.

As was suggested previously, Francis Warner also makes use of assonance and consonance as the basis of centre-rhyme.[1] On occasion, difficulties may arise in deciding what cases of sound parallelism should be counted as rhyming one with another. Assonances, in particular, easily escape the attention of the reader, if the gap between them is too wide, and tend to demand a careful analysis of the text in order to be discovered. However, the rhyming effect can be heightened considerably by the repetition of the vowel within the context of the line, so that a pattern of internal assonance is created which underscores the impact of the assonantal centre-rhyme. Alliteration and the

[1] According to Leech, *op. cit.*, p. 89, assonance is correspondence of vowels (e.g. gre*a*t/f*ai*l, s*e*nd/b*e*ll); consonance is correspondence of consonants (e.g. grea*t*/mea*t*, sen*d*/han*d*).

occasional use of end-rhyme provide further means of reinforce-
ment in lines where centre-rhyme is unobtrusive. Finally,
metrical stress frequently coincides with centre-rhymed elements
and thus helps to draw attention to 'weak' assonances.

Most of the devices noted above will be illustrated in the
following pages, where the rhyme pattern of an individual
poem will be examined in order to make concrete what might
otherwise be a mere abstraction. Sonnet XIX has been chosen
as a suitable specimen for analysis, because the poet's deploy-
ment of centre-rhyme here is unusually varied and complex. An
attempt will also be made to determine the function of centre-
rhyme within the poetic context as a whole, with special emphasis
on its rôle in the expression of theme and emotion.

II

Sonnet XIX

1 Night wins. The realizing dark
2 Granites that knife along eternity.
3 Who sins? What is this idle guilt?
4 Father forgive, by Thy Gethsemane.
5 Eat, drink, riot today and forget!
6 By Thine agony and bloody sweat—
7 Come, try at the wheel; spin, wager a bet!
8 Ransom my core from catastrophic debt.
9 If I must live with this full-earned abyss,
10 If I must face my moral holocaust
11 Father forgive, though I know what I do,
12 Forgive my sin against the Holy Ghost.
13   The worst is done; the last brutality:
14   And mine the sole responsibility.

Theme and emotion are one in this poem. In the opening
lines of the first quatrain the speaker's/the poet's growing aware-
ness of darkness and guilt reveals itself with keen intensity in the
image of approaching night. A second voice, which presumably
also represents the speaker of the poem, asks two rapid questions,
thus starting an argument which continues through the whole
of the second quatrain. This dialogue shows, in vivid flashes and
with strong emotional commitment, the speaker's ambivalence

in assuming full responsibility for his deed. The prayer 'Father forgive', already said in the first quatrain, is repeated and given further emphasis in the third quatrain, which makes way for the final acknowledgement of personal guilt in the couplet.

As far as centre-rhyme goes, the rhyme-scheme agrees with the pattern of *Type 1:* 121234565677 (see classification table above). Full rhyme alternates with assonance in the following way:

Lines 1 and 3
'Masculine' rhyme: wins/sins
Lines 2 and 4
Assonance: kn*i*fe/b*y* Th*y*
In line 4 the assonance in 'b*y* Th*y*' produces an internal rhyme. It is impossible in this case to tell which of the vowels should be counted as the main component of centre-rhyme, for, at least in my reading of the line, the difference of stress between the two syllables is very small.
Lines 5 and 7
'Feminine' rhyme: r*io*t/tr*y* at
When recited, these rhymes tend to become monosyllabic. This reading underlines the urgency of the second voice, which tries to persuade the hesitant first voice.
Lines 6 and 8
Double assonance: *a*g*o*ny/r*a*ns*o*m
The vowel sounds in 'r*a*ns*o*m' are echoed in 'c*a*t*a*str*o*phic'. To-gether these assonances form an internal rhyme.
Lines 9 and 11
'Masculine' rhyme: l*i*ve/forg*i*ve
Lines 10 and 12
Assonance: f*a*ce/ag*ai*nst
Lines 13 and 14 (= the couplet)
Polysyllabic end-rhyme: brutality/responsibility

The patterning of centre-rhyme has been made with a delicate feeling for the specific qualities of full rhyme and assonance respectively. In lines 1 and 3 the rhyme-words wins/sins estab-lish with acute immediacy the close relationship between the coming of night and the speaker's gradual realization of guilt. The rhyme pair riot/try at (lines 5 and 7) takes the theme of guilt a step further, suggesting two ways of escape from the fatal consequences of sin. In the third quatrain the rhyme-word 'forgive' (line 11), in particular, serves as an instrument in the thematic-emotional development, which resolves itself in the couplet and is given strong final emphasis by its end-rhyme: brutality/responsibility.

The assonances listed above have a complementary function in the evolution of theme and emotion. The double assonance of 'agony' and 'ransom' (lines 6 and 8) is the most prominent, partly because of the internal rhyme of 'ransom' and 'catastrophic' in line 8. The three words thus linked together are charged with thematic implications and, at the same time, they carry strong emotional overtones. The remaining assonances (lines 2 and 4, 10 and 12) are rather unobtrusive, but it should be noted that in these cases there is an approximate sound parallelism at the end of lines in eternity/Gethsemane (lines 2 and 4) and holocaust/ Holy Ghost (lines 10 and 12). In their contexts these word pairs invoke feelings associated with the theme of guilt.

Before making even a tentative assessment of the function of centre-rhyme in Sonnet XIX, I should like to point out two factors which complicate the rhyme pattern of this poem. One is that other forms of parallelism, such as verbal repetition and alliteration (for instance 'Father forgive' in lines 4 and 11 + 'Forgive' in line 12), undoubtedly also play an important rôle in the thematic-emotional context as a whole. Secondly, this sonnet, in effect, enacts a drama: throughout the poem two voices are heard debating an urgent moral question. This is a rather unusual cast for a sonnet, resulting in the creation of strong rhythmic tension in the second quatrain. The imperative orders in lines 5 and 7 actually threaten to violate the metric organization of the sonnet, but the poet's apt use of end-rhyme in this quatrain, in addition to centre-rhyme, prevents the impending disruption of the sonnet form. The vigorous rhyme-words forget/bet and sweat/debt all involve important semantic relationships which have a bearing on both theme and emotion.

Let us return then to the rôle of centre-rhyme in the wider poetic context of No. XIX. As was shown in the descriptive analysis made above, the majority of centre-rhymes are semantically relevant to the expression of theme and feeling. In cases of 'weak' assonance carefully chosen end-rhymes invoke emotional associations that support the thematic development. Furthermore, the effect of centre-rhyme is reinforced by metrical stress, which falls on most of the rhyming components.

In conclusion, it seems no exaggeration to claim that in Sonnet XIX the poet makes maximum use of rhyme as a significant structural unit. His rhyme technique adapts itself intimately to his preoccupation with guilt and the moral obligations of the 'sinner'. Thus the rich and perceptive orchestration of rhyme effects in this sonnet testifies not only to Francis Warner's inventiveness as a rhyme-maker but, what is more, to his remarkable poetic gifts.

LUCCA QUARTET

For Lorraine

Camaiore

Peace in the afternoon
   Sparkling eyes;
Sunbeams are rafters
   Stillness flies:
Wildwood contentment
   On hillside and path
Pinetree and olive
   Watch the hearth.

Farmyards of Tuscany
   Cupped in hills
Move in the shadows that
   Brightness fills.
Steep paths hesitate
   Stepping in green;
Dark wine for cover
   And lover's screen.

A baby is sleeping
   Through distant bells,
A bride in the valley sings.
   Smoke curls
From a weather-worn building
   Tiled in sun
Like your cheeks when happiness
   Is done.

Calm and elation
   Create this room.
One child paints flowers
   The other soon

Will call from the dusty track
   'Wake up! Let's start!'
Those years of your sadness
   Bred sweetness of heart.

May wings stretch over you
   Spring touch your vein
Loveliness lighten
   To childhood again
Falling hair fasten
   Love to your breast
By Florentine scentfall
   Caressed.

Choriambics

We are still wide-eyed awake. Come, shall we tread
                          out on the bare-foot paths
With the cool wind on our face? Yes, while no clothes
                          bother and night is ours.
We have both whispered so late eagerness sings
                          blood is alert. Next door
Two soft brushed children asleep, safe in shared warmth,
                          laid like sardines, secure
From all hobgoblins and fears, terrors and ticks,
                          giants and walking trees
That bedtime stories have spun, read with a last
                          bloodcurdling tender squeeze.
All the still valley's asleep. Cold in neat graves,
                          lit by electric coils,
The long past dead of the farms, cemetery snug,
                          glimmer their distant light,
While the stream washes, the breeze clouds out the moon.
                          Beauty, star of my sight,
Kiss me once more. Let us stay here
                          now, while the first bird calls.
In our flight far from the grey desolate days—
                          acres of years misspent—
We've discovered the best. Here let us rest
                          living complete content.

Canzone

Here sits the chess-set, silenced *in flagrante*
When your self-mocking anger
Mated checked love and challenged concentration.
Here sultry postcards, Carracci's Baccante
In tongue-tied exultation
And the Urbino Venus caught in languor,
Mother shocked stiff, scolding enough to hang her.
Here is the Elvis record, our reveille,
Lucy's sweet welcome crayoned for your breakfast—
They knew we always wake last
Dressing themselves and skipping down the valley.
Here are the trophies of our climbing zest
But what is goodness if we lack the best?

You have returned to face the storm-wind's music
With heightened trepidation
Branches of marriage falling in cold greeting.
What inner certainty drove you to choose it
A week from our first meeting
Turning all trials to wild exhilaration?
Spontaneous love's the father of creation.
When envy creeps up through our doors and shutters
Damning our sins, preaching anathemata
In hate of spring's cantata
Laughingly lived and sung past sneers and mutters,
Let us ignore caution's catastrophe
And breed proud children in shared ecstasy.

Madrigal

Will she ring, will she come? Children, what can I say?
I will wait as I've waited, indoors this springfresh day.
You must delight in the open, run, risk and dare
All the adventures of playtime. I will stay here.

Does she love, was she happy, wandering the world as ours?
Children, sunshine is brief in a lifetime of showers.
Our magic carpet was perfectest joy Fate can weave—
If now unravelled, little ones, we must not grieve.

Over the mountains, birdsong in Tuscany
Still haunts the leaftime, heightening memory.
Over the years such love will come your way.
Outside now, darlings. Please don't look. Just turn away.

Written 11–14 April 1975

Edward Malins

Lucca Quartet

In April 1975 Francis had not started on the last play of his double trilogy, which was to be performed at the Edinburgh Festival that autumn. So he decided he would try to take his two daughters abroad to some quiet place to get the job done during the Easter holiday. After mentioning his predicament to his friend Henry Moore, he was immediately offered Mary Moore's *casa colonica* at Camaiore in northern Tuscany for two weeks. It was an ideal season in which to go there. Browning, who knew the district well, described how

> You've summer all at once;
> In a day he leaps complete with a few strong April suns.

An ideal setting too: an old stone house, roughly plastered over, with shaded terrace, backed by extensive woodland, and over-looking the steep wooded hills, vineyards, and valleys of the Lucchese plain. Francis had long been attracted to Italy, like so many who read the Classics in the cold north, and having been there before, longed to know more of what Henry James called the 'Italian feeling, the Spirit of the South, and the vital principle of grace'. And no one understood the spirit of Tuscany with more exquisite sensibility than Henry James.

Ostensibly he was going there for two reasons: to write *Killing Time* and to give his children a happy time. Fate, however, decreed that he would not write a word, but that his children would much enjoy the trip. Cassius persuaded Brutus that 'Men at some time are masters of their fates', but that it is our own fault if we are 'underlings' of the gods. On this occasion Francis was an underling, for which we should be thankful, as we now have *Lucca Quartet* as well as *Killing Time*.

'Camaiore', the first poem of the *Lucca Quartet* (which is so called because there are four poems and four characters in them), describes the room in their house and the details of this *locus amoenus*: the bright afternoon sun lightens the large, rough beams of the ceiling, the children engaged in painting, the pines and olives as *lares* and *penates* of the hearth, the distant sounds of the village church bells and a girl singing all invest the scene with southern magic. The last two lines of the penultimate stanza bring in the fourth character, to whom the final stanza is addressed, his lover Lorraine, who had asked whether she might go with them. The poet calls for the wings of God to spread over her, like those in psalm XVII under which the psalmist asks to be hidden. And the stanza ends with a tender benediction to Lorraine—a falling cadence of gentle labial finality.

> Falling hair fasten
> Love to your breast
> By Florentine scentfall
> Caressed.

All is idyllic. Years of sadness have bred a sweetness in his lover's heart, and the poet sees her now set among 'Dark wine for cover / And lover's screen', which recalls the comforting words of the Chorus to the exiled Oedipus when they describe 'earth's loveliest of lands', the rich countryside of Colonus, to which Francis had taken his children in the summer of 1974:

> Screened in deep arbours, ivy, dark as wine,
> And tangled bowers of berry-clustered vine.

Perhaps 'Camaiore' might have been easier to read and nearer to this quiet peace had it been set up in quatrains of tetrameters in accordance with the rhyme scheme. The present arrangement of anapaestic and dactylic dimeters seems to make it fussy, though the final slow monosyllables to each of the three stanzas bestow the tranquillity which the poet feels she has brought with her.

> They from the throng of men had stepped aside,
> And made their home under the green hill-side.
> It was that hill, whose intervening brow
> Screens Lucca from the envious eye.

Thus did Shelley describe the wide valley of the Serchio river, which is overlooked by Pieve di Camaiore. In 'Choriambics' it is the hour before dawn in that same valley. The contemporary poet and his lover are wide awake, while the children sleep in the next room, safe after the fearsome bedtime stories of 'hob-goblins and fears, terrors and ticks' which had been read to them (C. S. Lewis, once Francis's tutor, would recognize *The Last Battle* from this description). But the dead are not far off, in the near-by cemetery and perhaps in 'the grey desolate days' of the Viet Nam war, for it happens that during that Easter weekend occurred some of the worst atrocities in that dreadful war. The polarity of love and war might be reading too much into the poem were it not for their close conjunction in *Killing Time*. For Francis, the gusset which joins the chain-mail of love and war is very real.

> Sleep, my little one. Hush!
> The guns chatter all night,
> Their flames are lively.
> Sleep, my little one,
> Soon you'll grow up and play with them.
> Hush, it is nothing, my little love,
> Close your ears, sleep, sleep,
> It's nothing, just life.

Yet in the final lines of the poem no anxiety about the future is shown; only the poet's wish to live 'in complete content', having 'discovered the best'. Throughout these poems we have no description or indication of the lineaments of the loved one, but, as Jon Stallworthy points out in his Introduction to *The Penguin Book of Love Poetry* (1973), that is not unusual. Neither Sappho, nor Catullus, Donne, Rochester, Byron, nor Graves ever has described in detail the physical features of their beloved: and Stallworthy gives the reason which I think applies in this case also. 'The poet in love and celebrating the fact is often writing for an audience of one; and all too often is only moved to define and describe his love more precisely when he has lost that audience or that vision.'

I know of no other modern English poet, except Rupert Brooke, who has used a choriambic metre. It provides a wonderful opportunity for monosyllabic spondees which lie so much at the very core of English verse; especially in this version of a choriambic metre in which there is more variety than in its classical model, in the use of an extra syllable in the final foot or sometimes transferred to the beginning of the line. An analysis

(at the risk of being akin to a C. S. Lewis tutorial) will show the
typical pattern:

While thĕ strēam | wāshĕs, thĕ brēeze | clouds out thĕ mōon |

If read aloud naturally, the counterpoint between the metre and
the natural rhythms of the sentence will bring out the melody.
One could continue at some length with such an analysis of this
poem, but I do not believe it would extend the reader's apprecia-
tion of the poem one jot. If he is interested he will find such
points as the *da capo* form of the poem, and the slowing down
and 'syncopation' as in the classical metre of the last line:

Wĕ've dĭs|cōvĕred thĕ bēst. | Hēre lĕt ŭs rēst | lĭvĭng cōmplēte |

(con)tēnt.

By the third poem of *Lucca Quartet* the two weeks' 'complete
content' is over, the lady has returned to face the 'storm wind's
music' of her failing marriage, and the poet dejectedly muses
like Coleridge upon 'Reality's dark dream' in his room at
Oxford. He looks round at objects which remind him of his
lover's presence: the chessmen left '*in flagrante*' in the middle of
a game; postcards of paintings they had seen together in the
Uffizi. Annibale Carracci's 'Bacchante' with its nude female
figure, and, appropriately in this case, the heads of two gazing
children, but, inaptly, the head of a satyr-like old man: and
Titian's bedded and reclining 'Urbino Venus', for which the
poet has accepted the explanation of a critic, who should know
better, that the girl's mother is scolding her for sexual im-
propriety. I need not say that the Elvis record is the poet's
daughters' choice rather than his own, and has as far as I know
no further significance. After this we read of homely details in
the children's life, and once again the somewhat vague reference
to the generic state of affairs which produces 'the best'. But all
is not well. The poet has heard envious and spiteful voices
which creep up 'through our doors and shutters' like death in
Jeremiah (again the link between love and death, to be de-
veloped in *Killing Time*.) Finally, in the manner of Dante in his
Canzoni, the postscript stating Francis's wish for marriage and
'proud children.'

The form of 'Canzone' follows the ancient lyric form which
Dante followed; it is in two equal parts of thirteen lines, each

having either seven or eleven syllables, and each rhyming word bound to another in the Canzone, including the first line with the last. If one cares to count, there are ten rhymes only, many of them of feminine rhymes as in the Italian models. I do not think that Francis speaks or writes Italian fluently, but he has evidently realized that many two-syllable rhymes in Italian are both melodious and commonly used, whereas in English they are rare because of possible triteness. Dante's Canzone 49 is evidently the nearest model for the *Lucca Quartet* 'Canzone'. The poet and his lover are parted and he wishes for death. It is worth quoting the first part of it:

> Quantunque volte, lasso, mi rimembra
> ch'io non debbo già mai
> veder la donna ond'io vo sì dolente,
>   tanto dolore intorno 'l cor m'assembra
> la dolorosa mente,
> ch'io dico: 'Anima mia, ché non ten vai?
>   ché li tormenti che tu porterai
> nel secol, che t'è già tanto noioso,
> mi fan pensoso di paura forte.'
> Ond'io chiamo la Morte,
> come soave e dolce mio riposo;
> e dico 'Vieni a me' con tanto amore,
> che sono astioso di chiunque more.

Alas, whenever I remember that I must never again see the lady on whose account I grieve, sorrowing memory brings such pain around my heart that I say: 'My soul, why do you not depart? For the suffering you will have to bear in this world— already so tedious to you—greatly oppresses my thoughts with fear.' So I call upon Death as my dear and sweet repose, and say: 'Come to me', with so much love that I am bitterly envious of all who die.[1]

This might all be of academic interest but that there must be few modern poets in English who are influenced by old poetic forms like canzoni. The poem is the most marked of the four in its personal utterance, that hall-mark of a romantic poet. We are interested in his spontaneous expression as a poet; his use of

[1] Trans. Foster and Boyde: *Dante's Lyric Poetry* (Oxford, 1967), pp. 88–9.

colloquial idiom and his personal subject all vitally contribute
to this.

A madrigal in poetry is usually a short, lyrical love song, and
Francis has already published a book of poems bearing that
title. All invariably could be set to music and the same title
retained. The final poem in *Lucca Quartet* deals with the questions
of the children to their father when they wonder whether
Lorraine will return. Inherently the questions show the pleasant
relationship that must have existed between them. Their father's
replies mostly show a philosophic stoicism about the whole
affair. Nevertheless the poem does not seem distanced, does not
appear recollected in tranquillity but too close to the happening
itself, and for that reason it seems the least successful of the four.
As usual the metrical scheme, derived through Campion and
Nashe from Italy and used successfully by them, has a classical
basis in its hurrying anapaests for the children's questions fol-
lowed by the slower beats for the replies. Even an anapaestic
first foot in Campion's

> Shall I come, sweet Love, to thee,
> When the ev'ning beames are set?

gives a pleasing contrast in the two parts of the line. So long as
metre and rhythms are appropriate to the mood of the poem, all
is well. Francis is a romantic poet, though he writes in his plays
of death, pain, and destruction. But even in his poems, the
proximity of death cannot be far from love, though it is clothed
in romantic words like *sunbeams, wildwood, flowers, moon, spring-
fresh, birdsong,* and *leaftime,* and these words are often happier in
a simple prosody suited to the natural scene of which he is so
conscious.

I am pleased to have permission to print here for the first
time a sonnet which is not part of the *Lucca Quartet* but which
was written between 'Canzone' and 'Madrigal' and is related
to the same theme. There is no difficulty in its interpretation,
for the final couplet shows how the relationship between the
poet and his lover is not finally established, but still consists of a
series of questions asked by him of her. It is a fine sonnet and it
could be said that the Shakespearian sonnet form, in which
Francis has written so frequently, suits him admirably, and in
many ways is more satisfactory than a more complex prosody.

Chesterton once wrote, 'One of the best tests in the world of what a poet means is in his metre', and there is no doubt of the tragedy in this sonnet, and the form perfectly matches the matter. Perhaps the tripping metres which Francis sometimes uses are reminiscent of Byron, who declared in his 'Stanzas for Music' that he was most unhappy, yet could write

There's not a joy the world can give like that it takes away.

Like Byron, Francis is an optimist, so the ultimate response conveyed in *Lucca Quartet* is optimistic, for the experience of the poet has been nurtured and celebrated. Let us hope he will give us more poems like *Lucca Quartet*.

Was it mere chance that brought the mating hare
Almost to touching distance as you stood
Still as a tree beside the sunlit wood
Downwind of him, your beagle nowhere near?
Were the white streaks along his whiskered cheeks
Furrows, too, caused by solitary tears?
Did his loose lope, his absence of all fears
Delight you? All his muddy scattering freaks?
Didn't you feel a happy naturalness
When his doe crossed the harrow to his side?
That all our Spring is blest, and has not died—
That deep love triumphs over danger's stress?
    Wasn't this vision in your saddest hours
    An emblem, darling, of what might be ours?

Contributors

Robert Burchfield C.B.E. is Editor of *A Supplement to the Oxford English Dictionary* and Chief Editor of the Oxford English Dictionaries.

Lesley Burnett is a graduate of Edinburgh University and had pursued post-graduate studies in Edinburgh and Oxford before joining the staff of *A Supplement to the Oxford English Dictionary*.

Suheil Bushrui is Professor of English and Anglo-Irish Literature at the American University of Beirut.

William Chapman was until recently Senior Scholar (Research) at Hertford College, Oxford.

Sorel Etrog is a Canadian sculptor.

Elisabeth Frink C.B.E. is a British sculptor.

Evie Garratt has created leading rôles in each of Warner's full-length plays.

Paul Hewison is Lecturer in English at the University of Aberdeen.

Sir Harold Hobson is our leading post-war drama critic.

Edward Malins is an authority on literature and landscaping. His publications include *English Landscaping and Literature 1660–1840* (Oxford), *A Preface to Yeats* (Longmans), and, with the Knight of Glin, *Lost Demesnes, Irish Landscape Gardening 1660–1845* (Barrie and Jenkins).

Ingrid Melander is Assistant Professor of English Literature at the University of Umeå, Sweden. Her doctoral thesis, *The Poetry of Sylvia Plath. A Study of Themes*, was published in 1972.

Melinda Camber Porter is Paris Correspondent and Arts Feature Writer for *The Times*.

Tim Prentki is a tutor for the Oxford University Department for External Studies. His first play was performed last year.

Glyn Pursglove is Lecturer in English at the University of Wales at Swansea.

David Self writes for *Plays and Players* and the *Times Educational Supplement*, and for radio and television.